**explore**

Nineteen Eighty-Four

George Orwell

Guide written by Claire Crane
and Juliet Walker

 **A** *Letts* **Literature Guide for GCSE**

Contents

Contents

Plot summary

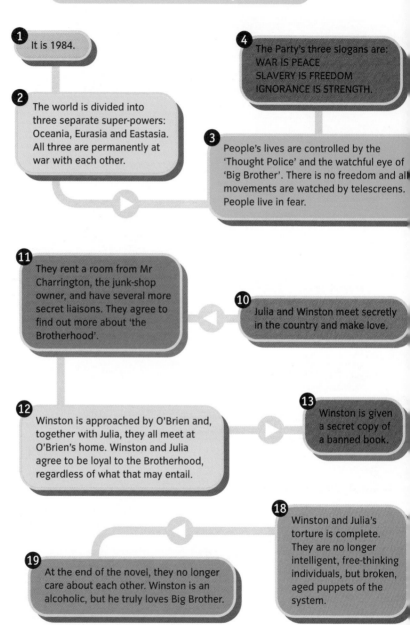

1 It is 1984.

2 The world is divided into three separate super-powers: Oceania, Eurasia and Eastasia. All three are permanently at war with each other.

4 The Party's three slogans are:
WAR IS PEACE
SLAVERY IS FREEDOM
IGNORANCE IS STRENGTH.

3 People's lives are controlled by the 'Thought Police' and the watchful eye of 'Big Brother'. There is no freedom and all movements are watched by telescreens. People live in fear.

11 They rent a room from Mr Charrington, the junk-shop owner, and have several more secret liaisons. They agree to find out more about 'the Brotherhood'.

10 Julia and Winston meet secretly in the country and make love.

12 Winston is approached by O'Brien and, together with Julia, they all meet at O'Brien's home. Winston and Julia agree to be loyal to the Brotherhood, regardless of what that may entail.

13 Winston is given a secret copy of a banned book.

18 Winston and Julia's torture is complete. They are no longer intelligent, free-thinking individuals, but broken, aged puppets of the system.

19 At the end of the novel, they no longer care about each other. Winston is an alcoholic, but he truly loves Big Brother.

5 Winston Smith is an average, middle-aged Outer Party worker, who dreams of a better world, but is too oppressed to do anything about it.

7 Winston catches O'Brien's eye one day, and remembers a dream he had in which this Inner Party member told him: 'We will meet in the place where there is no darkness.'

6 Winston works in the Ministry of Truth, faking past documents and changing the way history is recorded.

8 Inspired by O'Brien, and in a minor act of rebellion, Winston buys a diary and an old-fashioned ink-pen to write down his thoughts. This is a treasonable offence.

9 After spotting her, and being suspicious of her, on several occasions, Winston eventually talks to Julia – a co-worker. She passes him a note which reads 'I love you'.

4 After another liaison at Mr Charrington's, Julia and Winston are shocked when they hear a voice. The room is bugged and they are arrested by armed men. Mr Charrington is a member of the Thought Police.

15 They are taken to the Ministry of Love and tortured by O'Brien until they confess their crimes.

17 Unable to stop himself, he denounces Julia in a final act of betrayal.

16 Winston's torture is detailed and complex and he is eventually taken to Room 101, where he meets his greatest fear – rats!

Who's who in *Nineteen Eighty-Four*

Winston Smith

Winston Smith, the central character of the novel, is <u>not a typical</u> <u>hero-figure</u>. He is a lonely individual, fairly small and slight, in <u>poor</u> <u>physical</u> <u>condition</u>, and does not consider himself attractive. He is surprised at Julia's interest in a physical relationship with him. His <u>lack of</u> <u>confidence</u> (both in himself and his world) is such that he is unsure what to write in his diary and even uncertain as to what year it really is. He works in the Ministry of Truth, where <u>his job</u> – '<u>his</u> <u>greatest</u> <u>pleasure</u> <u>in</u> <u>life</u>' – is to alter publications to fit in with the Party's presentation of events. Although he does not approve of this obliteration of the past, he works conscientiously and takes <u>intellectual</u> pride in doing his job well, particularly the 'intricate and responsible' tasks.

Winston is a <u>sensitive</u> man, who appreciates the few beautiful objects left in an ugly society and who has a deep affinity with the natural world. He <u>despises</u> <u>ugliness</u> <u>of</u> <u>behaviour</u> in himself, such as joining in the Two Minutes Hate, even though he cannot help himself. Later, however, he is willing to undertake far more horrific acts as a condition of joining the Brotherhood. He feels the need to <u>confess</u> unpleasant behaviour towards his mother and sister when he was a boy and to try to cleanse himself by writing about his experience with a middle-aged prole prostitute. Winston's <u>contemplative</u> nature is really his downfall, for he is not prepared to accept the lies of the Party.

What most horrifies Winston is the <u>hiding</u> <u>of</u> <u>truth</u>, and he is very troubled by the Party's motives in changing history, as indicated by the capitalisation of adverbs: '<u>I</u> <u>understand</u> <u>HOW:</u> I <u>do</u> <u>not</u> <u>understand</u> <u>WHY</u>'. For years before his quiet rebellion of starting the diary, 'an interminable restless monologue' has been running inside his head. The external manifestation of this is the <u>varicose ulcer</u> on his leg, which is a symbol of his dissatisfaction. The ulcer itches and throbs at moments of frustration and virtually disappears when he falls in love with Julia. After his imprisonment, torture and humiliation it becomes 'an inflamed mass'.

Winston is <u>fatalistic</u> and knows from the beginning that he will be caught and that he is already one of '<u>the dead</u>', but Julia's love for him gives him the incentive to survive for as long as possible. Despite this he takes risks, though he cannot be held entirely responsible for his own downfall as the Thought Police have put temptation in his way for years. We are told that, 'For some reason the telescreen in the living room was in an unusual position'. The 'reason' is surely so that Winston can be encouraged to write his diary, hidden in an alcove – a diary that a member of the Thought Police has sold to him. He is <u>doomed</u> before the novel starts. He <u>hides</u> <u>from</u> <u>himself</u> things that he has the intelligence to see clearly. For example, it suits him to trust O'Brien, to whom he writes his 'interminable letter' (the diary). Since Julia is not his intellectual equal and switches off or falls asleep when the conversation becomes political, he sees O'Brien as someone sympathetic with whom he can communicate. Ultimately it does not matter to Winston whether O' Brien is a friend or enemy.

Winston plays the <u>role</u> of devoted Party member, while being a <u>secret</u> <u>rebel</u>, and he is fascinated by the idea of <u>disguise</u> (as was Orwell). The painted face of the prostitute, 'like a mask', appeals to him. He does not, however, think deeply about other people who may be acting out roles.

Although the novel is written in the <u>third</u> <u>person</u>, everything is seen from Winston's point of view. We have his impression of characters and events, so do not always see the whole picture. Although we are <u>misled</u> by his misjudgement of some events – for example thinking that it will be Mrs Parsons who will be vaporized

– it is an effective narrative technique to show the horror of the totalitarian state through the experiences of an individual with whom we have some sympathy and understanding. One title that Orwell considered for the book was *The Last Man in Europe* – that is, the last clear-thinking man – bringing the focus firmly onto Winston. Do you think we still sympathise with Winston at the end, after he has been brainwashed?

What is the significance of Winston's name? The name is oxymoronic, for it contains contradictory impressions. 'Winston' is very specific, setting him apart, and 'Smith' is the most common surname in England, making him a kind of Everyman. To contemporary readers, 'Winston' would automatically have signalled Churchill, who had just led the country through World War Two. Churchill was defeated in parliament in 1945, probably the year of Winston's birth, so perhaps the choice of name is ironic, signifying ultimate downfall; or perhaps it reflects his courage and determination in the face of the enemy. It is hard to be sure what Orwell intended, for in his many writings he was sometimes very critical of Churchill and sometimes full of admiration, but we can be sure that he did not give the name randomly; after all, he thought carefully about how he was going to present himself to the world as George Orwell rather than Eric Blair.

Julia

Julia is a young woman, about 27 years old. She is described as a 'bold-looking girl', attractive, with 'dark hair, a freckled face and swift, athletic movements'. Her charisma provokes an uncomfortable feeling in Winston, which he initially understands to be hatred. It is, in fact, the opposite. She works as a technician in a special department of Minitrue, producing cheap pornography for the proles, and seems to embody the image of a true Party member, with her scarlet sash – the emblem of the

Junior Anti-Sex League – which she wears permanently. Julia exudes the healthy vigour of 'hockey-fields and cold baths and community hikes and general clean-mindedness'.

She is confident, practical and a risk-taker and enjoys taking the lead. It is Julia who first approaches Winston, and she is very matter-of-fact about arranging their secret meetings. We discover that she has already had several illicit love affairs and uses sex for fun as well as for rebellion. She is happy to steal make-up and perfume to fuel Winston's fantasies. Unlike Winston, she is willing to accept the overnight changes in Oceania's history and although she hates the Party, she has no interest in criticising its doctrine. She refuses to use Newspeak, and she does not believe in the existence of the Brotherhood.

Julia presents a striking contrast to Winston, and their love affair initially seems hard to believe. Physically, they are very different, and Julia is also down-to-earth and passionate. Winston describes her as being 'a rebel from the waist downwards'. Although she is not a great political thinker, she has an innate intelligence, which enables her to follow her own course. She understands the need to give the appearance of toeing the Party line and she is actively involved in various societies and meetings, which she also encourages Winston to take part in. She understands how the Party manipulates people's natural, sexual desires and channels them into hatred against Big Brother's enemies.

We get the impression that Julia is stronger than Winston and she is certainly the first to tell O'Brien that they will never be separated. At the end of the novel she admits that she betrayed Winston and the physical change in her is shocking. Her face is 'sallower' and she has a long scar across her forehead. She seems to have 'stiffened' and we get the impression that she is now frozen, both physically and mentally. She reminds Winston of a corpse, and certainly the life that she once had appears to have been extinguished.

O'Brien

O'Brien is a high-ranking and highly intelligent member of the <u>Inner</u> <u>Party</u>, who is only seen from Winston's point of view. He apparently works in the Ministry of Truth, but it is revealed in Part III that his major role is in the Ministry of Love as an <u>inquisitor</u> of prisoners accused of thoughtcrime. After Winston, O'Brien is the character with the most prominent role in the novel; he is mentioned in the first chapter, but his major contribution is in the final, intense chapters, when Winston is interrogated, tortured and re-integrated into the Party. It is O'Brien's <u>fanatical</u> <u>intelligence</u> which ultimately defeats Winston, though O'Brien considers it as saving him.

O'Brien's distinctive – and <u>deceptive</u> – appearance and mannerisms are frequently mentioned. He is 'a large, burly man with a thick neck and a coarse, humorous, brutal face'. He has '<u>a certain charm</u>' of manner and is <u>graceful</u> in his bulkiness. Winston finds his mannerism of resettling his spectacles on his nose '<u>curiously civilised</u>' – a quality generally absent from this culture – and 'curiously disarming'; in other words, removing feelings of suspicion and hostility. It is revealingly described as a '<u>trick</u>', suggesting it is calculated and designed to deceive. This is similar to the way he '<u>manipulates</u>' a cigarette, the verb emphasising his <u>skilful</u> <u>control</u>, both of the cigarette and of Winston.

O'Brien is cunning in the way that he presents himself to Winston as an enigmatic character who might be <u>friend</u> <u>or</u> <u>foe</u>. Winston recognises that there is '<u>a</u> <u>link</u> <u>of</u> <u>understanding</u>' between them – he even features in his dreams – and O'Brien admits that he enjoys talking to Winston, because they have <u>similar</u> <u>minds</u>. He seems to know what Winston is thinking and has been patiently watching his target for 7 years. He cleverly <u>traps</u> him by fleetingly catching his eye during the Two Minutes Hate (with his glasses removed) and by contriving a meeting in the Ministry of Truth corridor, almost exactly where Julia gives him her note. He is the one who provides the missing lines from the 'Oranges and Lemons' rhyme, when the time is right. He manages, in a chant-like exchange, to extract from Winston the agreement to commit atrocious crimes in the name of the Brotherhood, a fact which he later uses against him. He is a skilful actor, who sometimes assumes an unthreatening 'absent-minded' attitude. It is ironic that Winston thinks that it is the servant, Martin, who is the one playing a role. O'Brien deliberately echoes Winston's words, 'We are the dead', which should give away that his entire conversation with Julia in Charrington's room has been overheard, but presumably O'Brien takes the risk that Winston will take this as a sign of like-thinking and solidarity.

O'Brien appears almost fatherly towards Winston when he interrogates him; he talks about watching over him and saving him. He speaks gently and is compared to a doctor, teacher or priest, who is 'anxious to explain and persuade, rather than punish', yet he readily has the dial turned up high to inflict pain when he deems it necessary. The fanatical side – the real side – of O'Brien does not fully appear until the latter stages of his interrogation of Winston, when he shows 'lunatic enthusiasm'. Despite this, Winston still respects O'Brien's mind as being far superior to his own. O'Brien inspires admiration, almost worship, and is seen as 'invincible' – a physical manifestation, almost, of Big Brother.

Mr Charrington

Charrington is a member of the Thought Police, working undercover, though this is not discovered until his last appearance at the end of Part II. He is the 63-year-old proprietor of 'a frowsy little junk-shop' in the prole district.

Charrington looks harmless and unthreatening. The narrator uses adjectives associated with kindness and gentleness to describe him: his eyes are 'mild', his long nose 'benevolent' and his voice 'soft'. The clues are there, because his eyes are 'distorted by thick spectacles' and he has 'bushy' black eyebrows contrasting with his white hair, both details suggesting disguise. He is in costume to act his part convincingly, his black velvet jacket making him seem educated, a detail which would appeal to the thoughtful Winston. His accent is not as coarse as that of most proles, which should raise alarm bells.

Charrington cunningly gains Winston's confidence by flattering his taste in collectable objects. He is clever not to push too far though, just to plant ideas in Winston's head. He sells him the paperweight, and his offer to show Winston the goods in a room upstairs is also a way of entrapping him. He stage manages the visit, so that the room is appealing with its 'warm dim light'. It is Charrington who brings up the subject of 'Oranges and Lemons' with its ominous last line: 'Here comes a chopper to chop off your head', which he repeats coldly when Winston and Julia are captured.

Charrington is not judgmental and appears to do everything to make the room safe and private for Julia and Winston. He makes himself unobtrusive, by 'seeming almost to fade out of existence'. It is strange that he barely has any other customers and leads 'a ghostlike existence', as if he is only on view when Winston needs him. Winston fails to see that he is too good to be true.

Charrington is eventually unmasked during the couple's arrest. He undergoes a number of changes: his voice becomes 'thin' and 'cultivated', his hair is black and the glasses have been removed. He now has 'an alert, cold face' of a man of about 35.

Like most of Orwell's characters, his name could have several connotations. It might suggest Charrington beer, a real product, that the proles may have drunk. In a more sinister way, it also carries an echo of Charon, the mythological ferryman who carried dead souls to the Underworld. Certainly Charrington is responsible for Winston's journey to a hellish place.

Parsons

Tom Parsons is Winston's <u>neighbour</u> at Victory Mansions and <u>co-worker</u> at the Ministry of Truth. He is a 'tubby, middle-sized man with fair hair and a froglike face'. He is described as 35 years old and permanently sweaty, partly due to his 'rolls of fat', and partly because he seems to rush everywhere in a 'brisk and boyish' fashion. He has a childish air about him and gives the impression that he is constantly wearing shorts and a neckerchief. He is not held in much esteem, either by the intellectual Syme, who thinks him a '<u>bloody fool</u>', or by Winston, who despises him for his <u>blind</u> <u>acceptance</u> of everything the Party tells him. Parsons is active in the community groups, taking a lively role in decorating the flats for Hate Week, for example. Because of his <u>slavish</u> <u>loyalty</u> to Big Brother and his adoration (and slight nervousness) about his own children's vicious actions in the Spies, Winston assumes Parsons will never be vaporized.

After Parsons has been arrested. Winston is shocked to see his neighbour, '<u>blubbering</u>' and accused of '<u>thoughtcrime</u>'. Despite being denounced by his own daughter for calling out 'Down with Big Brother' in his sleep, he is still pathetically loyal to the Party and maintains that he must have been guilty: '<u>You</u> <u>don't</u> <u>think</u> <u>the</u> <u>Party</u> <u>would</u> <u>arrest</u> <u>an</u> <u>innocent</u> <u>man,</u> <u>do</u> <u>you?</u>' Even though his terror causes him to lose control of his bowels in the cell, he insists that he bears his daughter no grudge and is '<u>proud</u> <u>of</u> <u>her</u>', because it shows he '<u>brought</u> <u>her</u> <u>up</u> <u>in</u> <u>the</u> <u>right</u> <u>spirit</u>'.

Parsons represents a typically devoted and <u>brainwashed</u> member of society: patriotic, unthinking and loyal. Despite these qualities, however, Orwell shows us that the Party is indiscriminate in those it chooses to make into <u>victims</u>. Parsons illustrates the fact that in the world of *Nineteen Eighty-Four*, it is impossible to be a model citizen and that the long arm of Big Brother will strike at even the most unlikely candidate, thus increasing paranoia and fear.

Big Brother

Big Brother is an important symbol, but is never actually seen, and may even be invented by the Party. Nevertheless, Big Brother dominates Oceania in *Nineteen Eighty-Four*. He is <u>ever</u> <u>present</u> and seemingly <u>omnipotent</u>, watching down on everyone from posters, banners and telescreens. He is never seen in person, only via the media, and has a <u>striking appearance</u>: 'black haired', 'black moustachio'd', and 'ruggedly handsome'. His <u>eyes</u> are <u>hypnotic</u> and '<u>scrutinise</u>' you, with the uncanny knack of following you around. They create the effect of 'some huge force ... battering against your brain, frightening you out of your beliefs'. His face is vast and is deliberately the only colour in the grey, leaden world. It is cleverly presented as being '<u>full</u> <u>of</u> <u>power</u>' yet also having '<u>mysterious</u> <u>calm</u>'. The smile is ambiguous.

His posters carry the words '<u>BIG</u> <u>BROTHER</u> <u>IS</u> <u>WATCHING</u> <u>YOU</u>', and while the term 'brother' suggests a cosy, comrade-like companion, this could not be further from the truth. In essence, Big Brother is a <u>god-like</u> being who dominates his followers. He is described as 'invincible, fearless' and as a 'protector' who exudes 'wisdom and majesty'. Orwell uses Big Brother as a <u>symbol</u> <u>of</u> <u>powerful</u> <u>dictators</u>, such as Stalin (who even looked like Big Brother), Hitler, Franco and Mussolini. For Party members he has the power to incite devotion, but he is also used as the ultimate threat. For the proles he is a distant authority figure.

The proles

The proles are the underclass, the bottom strata of society. They have more freedom than members of the Outer Party, like Winston, because they are thought not to have the intelligence to rebel. The Party slogan, 'Proles and animals are free', sums up the regime's opinion of them. They can go to the pub for their entertainment, rather than to community meetings, and are able to have relationships without Party interference. They live in squalid surroundings, where crime of every sort is rife, and they are kept under control by rocket bombs. There are few telescreens in the prole district, but there are Thought Police patrols, which eliminate anyone who shows political tendencies. They are issued with material that the Party sees as appropriate for them, including computer-generated catchy songs and pornography. They speak in clichéd cockney accents and the ones we see closely, like the old man in the pub, are caricatures. Despite Winston's views, it is hard to imagine rebellion coming from this area of society.

Pyramidal hierarchy in Oceania in 1984

Big Brother

Party figurehead

O'Brien
Charrington

(from the past:
Jones, Aaronson, Rutherford;
exiled: Emmanuel Goldstein)

The Inner Party
(less than 2% of population)

Winston Smith
Julia
Parsons
Ampleforth   Colleagues in the
Syme   Ministry of Truth
Tillotson
Wilsher

Mrs Parsons and the two children; Bumstead,
the prisoner (from the past; Winston's mother
and sister and his wife, Katharine)

The Outer Party
(13% of population)

Mr Charrington, when working undercover   Old man in pub
Woman 'Smith' in prison   Woman singing while
Martin, O'Brien's servant   hanging up washing

The proles (85% of population)

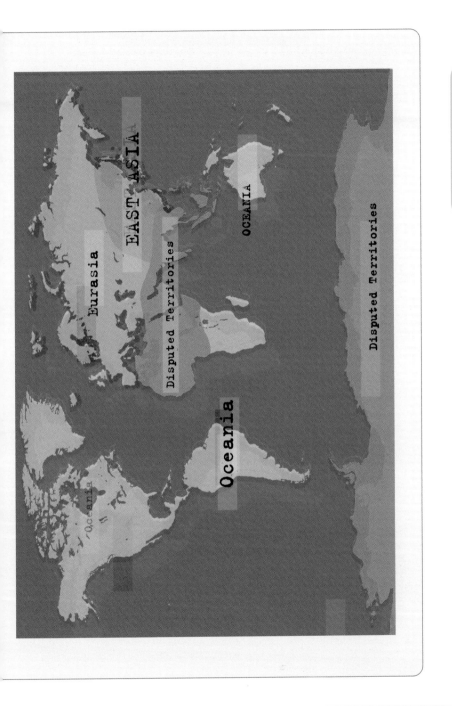

Eurasia

EAST ASIA

Disputed Territories

OCEANIA

Disputed Territories

Oceania

Oceania

About the author

George Orwell

George Orwell, a name assumed for writing purposes in the 1930s, was born Eric Arthur Blair in India in June 1903. His relatively short life was varied and active, despite being dogged by illness. Many of his experiences now sound much stranger than fiction. He was also an unusual looking man, very tall and gangly at 6 feet 4 inches, and not always comfortable socially.

He had a privileged public school education at Eton College, but decided not to go to Oxford University. He enrolled in the Indian Imperial Police Force, enduring a posting to Burma for 5 years. He returned home to become a writer – a childhood ambition – which caused a rift in his disapproving family.

Orwell felt a great amount of guilt as a young man (partly because of his moneyed background), and in an attempt to come to terms with this and to understand the depths of society, he spent some time living among tramps and outcasts in London. At one time he slept in Trafalgar Square wrapped in newspaper. Orwell's friends said that he did not look convincing in the role of a tramp, because of his great height, moustache and military bearing. He wrote about his experiences in his first book, *Down and Out in Paris and London*.

While trying to make a living from writing, Orwell took various jobs, including dishwashing in Paris, childminding, hop picking, teaching (which he considered 'foul') and shopkeeping. In the 1930s he fought for the Republicans in the Spanish Civil War. When he wrote about this experience later, he commented on the manipulation of history. He also became aware of censorship and propaganda during his time broadcasting on BBC radio during World War Two. Such observations were stored up for later use in *Nineteen Eighty-Four*.

Orwell wrote in many genres and was always admired more for his ideas than for his style. He was an atheist, held socialist views and had a sharp political mind. He did not gain wide recognition until the publication of *Animal Farm* in 1945. *Nineteen Eighty-Four* was his last novel, published in 1949, and written when he was dying from the lung disease tuberculosis. This partly explains its depressing tone; he told a friend that it was more pessimistic than he intended.

Orwell married twice, first in 1936 and secondly 3 months before his death, when he was confined to bed in the last stages of his illness. His first wife died only a few months after they had adopted a baby, but Orwell did his best to care for the boy, with the help of his sister. Before he became too ill, they were living on Jura, a sparsely inhabited Scottish island, which was where he finished writing *Nineteen Eighty-Four*.

Orwell died in early 1950. His writing is still very much alive – his books have sold more than 40 million copies and gain new readers every year, not all of them studying his novels for GCSE! Phrases from *Nineteen Eighty-Four* have entered the language, for example 'Big Brother' and 'Room 101'. 2003 saw a rise in sales of Orwell's books, because of the interest generated by the anniversary of his birth.

> *Every line of serious work that I have written since 1936 has been written, directly or indirectly, against totalitarianism.*

Orwell was interested in political movements, something he had already explored in the communist satire *Animal Farm*. In *Nineteen Eighty-Four* it is totalitarianism that is the main target. In some of his earlier essays and writings he had given warning of future political dangers. For Orwell, the preservation of truth and freedom of thought were supremely important. From the 1930s, particularly in his experiences of the Spanish Civil War, he saw the seeds of the regime he later portrayed in *Nineteen Eighty-Four*. He also incorporated aspects of totalitarian Russia, under the dictator Stalin, including show trials, children betraying parents, the worship of a figurehead and Five Year Plans.

A totalitarian political system is one in which those in power have absolute control and do not allow any form of opposition. This sort of regime breeds distrust in its citizens, which leads to suspicion and betrayal, even of family and friends. This was especially true of Russia between the two World Wars and, to a lesser extent, Italy and Germany in the mid-1930s. The case of Russia, particularly, provides many parallels with the world of *Nineteen Eighty-Four*. Stalin (Big Brother), the successor of Lenin, gradually ousted other leading revolutionary leaders (members of the Inner Party), particularly Trotsky (Emmanuel Goldstein), and had total control by 1928. He was image-conscious, making sure that he appeared in photographs as taller and more robust than he really was, in order to seem an ideal leader. Five Year Plans meant that businesses and factories had to try to meet ridiculously high targets. Failure to do so could result in execution (vaporization). Rebels were sent to slave labour camps and many thousands, including scientists and poets (Ampleforth) disappeared in the purges. In the 1930s, Stalin began rewriting history. School books and encyclopaedias were altered or destroyed (Ministry of Truth).

Cultural context

In the early 1950s, readers had a very different perspective on the novel than we do today. Orwell's vision of the future may well have seemed like a very real prospect. Readers had just come through World War Two. It was still a time of rationing, and so certain aspects of Winston's life would have struck a chord.

In 1984, however, readers would have had another view – one tempered by relief that Orwell's vision had not come true. Today, although this warning has not transpired, there is more evidence of Big Brother watching us than there ever was in the 1980s, with electronic tagging of criminals, closed-circuit television, satellite surveillance, DNA fingerprinting and RFID (Radio Frequency Identification) used in shopping tags.

The novel is a science fiction dystopia. While a utopia is an imaginary place of ideal perfection, a dystopia is the complete opposite. The ideas, rather than the plot or characterisation, are what drive this book.

St Clement Dane Church. An image of this church, still standing in London and mentioned in the nursery rhyme 'Oranges and Lemons', is in Charrington's upstairs room.

Themes and images

Loss of freedom

As in any totalitarian regime, those in power (the Party and Big Brother) maintain absolute control through a rigid command over the lives of the people, especially those in the Outer Party. Such control means that virtually all the types of freedom that we take for granted are automatically forfeit: 'You had to live in the assumption that every sound you made was overheard, and, except in darkness, every movement scrutinised.'

The luxury of privacy is lost due to the ubiquitous presence of the telescreens. Not only do they peer at citizens in their own homes, but they are also positioned in the streets, while microphones are concealed in the countryside. The telescreens are also a means by which commands can be shouted at individuals, as Winston discovers when he is not exercising hard enough at the start of the novel. Harmless pleasures, such as being able to keep a diary or being able to have free time are also lost in *Nineteen Eighty-Four*. Winston feels sure that the act of writing in his diary could lead to 25 years in a forced labour camp. In addition, it is expected that the majority of time spent outside work is to be devoted to working for the good of the Party, attending meetings or joining a society: 'in principle a Party member had no spare time'. The idea of having 'ownlife' is a freedom that is not permitted.

Because happiness and love are distracting emotions, another freedom that the Party has tried to abolish is the idea of falling in love and being happily married. Suitable wives and husbands are selected by the Party, and any joy or physical happiness is eradicated by systematic brainwashing of young women through the efforts of the Junior Anti-Sex League.

Perhaps the most ruthless loss of freedom for most individuals, however, is the liberty to have private thoughts. Winston treasures his dreams and his opinions, but he knows he would be punished for 'thoughtcrime' if they were discovered.

The very term 'Thought Police' suggests that Big Brother is capable of reading minds, and that any stray, unacceptable notions are the equivalent of a serious crime and result in appropriate punishment. Winston says in Chapter VII: 'Freedom is the freedom to say that two plus two make four. If that is granted, all else follows.' Of course, in Oceania, this freedom is not granted. Newspeak is one tool used by Big Brother to limit private thoughts. The view is that if the vocabulary for expressing improper beliefs is not available, after a time people will not have the thoughts in the first place. By the end of the novel, after being tortured and brainwashed, it is significant that Winston aimlessly traces in the dust of the café table '$2 + 2 = 5$'. His absolute loss of freedom has been achieved, mentally as well as physically. All his actions and views are now controlled by the Party.

Violence

Violence and aggression pervade the novel, from the ruins of the war-strewn society described in Chapter I, to the broken, tortured characters of Winston and Julia in the final chapter. Big Brother and the Party encourage aggression and war-like emotions in all citizens of Oceania, even to the extent of channelling these violent tendencies in a daily 'Two Minutes Hate', wherein people are expected to vent their fury in a mob-like scene of accepted socially violent behaviour.

Orwell describes a typical Two Minutes Hate in Chapter I, so we are in no doubt as to the importance of this ritual. He describes the mood as a 'frenzy' and a 'hideous ecstasy'. People are 'flushed' and Winston explains how it induces a 'desire to kill, to torture, to smash faces in with a sledge-hammer'. What is most disturbing about this scene, apart from the fact that it is condoned, is the mingling of hostility and sexual tension. 'Ecstasy' and 'desire' indicate that in this world aggression has replaced tenderness, and love has been eradicated by hate. This notion is developed when Winston's initial thoughts about Julia, to whom he is attracted, are to 'flog her to death' before tying her 'naked to a stake' and then brutally raping her, just before cutting her throat. These are terrifying images for the reader to accept.

Violence is also actively encouraged in the children of Oceania, who belong to 'The Spies' – a violent Hitler-Youth type organisation. Winston's meeting with one of Parsons children illustrates the casual use of aggression which is expected of them: 'something hit the back of his neck an agonisingly painful blow. It was as though a red-hot wire had been jabbed into him'. It is the result of a catapult blow, but the perpetrator is not admonished by his mother. She merely looks frightened of the boy.

Everyday activities are similarly suffused with this violent atmosphere. When Winston walks through the slum district he is knocked sideways by one of the constant rocket bombs, and is so used to seeing victims blown apart that when he comes across a torn limb, he kicks the 'thing' unceremoniously into a gutter.

Of course, the most frightening violence of all is that hinted at by the constant threat of the Thought Police. Like all things unknown, the fear is all-pervasive and horrifying. It is significant that after Winston and Julia are finally arrested – an act heralded by physical agony, for Julia is punched in the stomach and Winston feels 'deadly pain' – Winston's actual torture is not described in detail. As readers we are only allowed access to the results of it – his physical degeneration. What finally makes Winston succumb is simply the threat of the rats and the hurt they may cause him.

Even Winston's hopes for a new future with the Brotherhood are charged with brutality, as we see when O'Brien tests his loyalty by asking what terrible acts of violence he is prepared to undertake: 'If, for example, it would serve our interests to throw sulphuric acid in a child's face – are you prepared to do that?' This demonstrates that in the world of *Nineteen Eighty-Four*, even redemption is not free from aggression. The cruelty of the Party is summed up by O'Brien, in his real guise, when he urges Winston to visualise the future: 'imagine a boot stamping on a human face – for ever'.

Nature

There is much readily accessible natural imagery running through the novel, from the 'beetle-like' men with 'scuttling' movements, to the Parsons children who gambol 'like tiger cubs which will soon grow up into man-eaters'. However, the main function of nature, like the past, is to show an ideal world – what the world used to be like and could still be like, were the Party to be overthrown.

The motif of The Golden Country is the main representation of this. This landscape is seen as perfect and bountiful, with all of the sunny connotations of gold but none of the associated greed. It is the landscape of Winston's dreams, but seems completely real to him, even though he may never have visited it as a boy. The name suggests the phrase 'The Golden Age', an imagined time when life was idyllic. The Golden Country serves as a total contrast to the sterile capital, 'vast and ruinous, city of a million dustbins'. The natural elements of earth, air, water and fire are all used to stress the life-enhancing qualities of the country. Winston notes that 'the air seemed to kiss one's skin'; the stream water is clear and contains fish; the ground is 'short springy turf', home to moles and rabbits; and the sun gilds the ground.

This is a naturally colourful environment, while the city is monochrome apart from the Big Brother posters and the scarlet sashes of the Junior Anti-Sex League. Symbolically, Julia flings her sash away from her in the countryside. Winston's wife, Katharine, who felt uncomfortable in the country unless they were in a group on an organised hike, could never have behaved like this. When Orwell writes about the Golden Country the language becomes lyrical with a suggestion of watery movement: there is 'dappled light and shade', 'pools of gold', and the ground 'misty with bluebells'.

Winston and Julia hear a thrush singing full-throatedly, just for the sake of it. The song has such a profound effect on Winston that 'He stopped thinking and merely felt'. It is this song which unlocks his inhibitions and enables him to defy the Party further by making love with Julia. He mentions the thrush to Julia just before their arrest, reminded of it by the spontaneous singing of the prole woman. It is perhaps a hint that natural emotions will survive somewhere, despite the Party's effort to destroy them.

After this episode there are no more glimpses of the Golden Country. London has 'interminable winters' and natural life in the park, where Winston runs into Julia, is shown as stunted, with 'not a bud anywhere'. This lack of new growth provides a depressing end to the novel. The inappropriately named Chestnut Tree Café is 'an ill-omened' place. The spreading branches, which should offer shelter and protection, only offer limitless doses of bitter gin and a brief respite before the inevitable bullet.

The past

'Who controls the past controls the future: who controls the present controls the past.' The past, something that Winston is striving to understand, remember and retain, is an important theme, explored through dreams, memories, rhymes, Party policies and the few remaining beautiful objects. Winston's job is to alter the past in printed records, but he is on a personal quest to find out the truth. This leads him to questioning an old man in a pub, exploring a junk shop and trying to find out the missing lines from the rhyme 'Oranges and Lemons' about the bells of old London churches. The past is elusive, but has not been completely erased.

Accurate knowledge of the past is one of the things that the totalitarian regime of Oceania denies its citizens, considering this necessary for the Party's stability. People must be proficient at doublethink and conquer their own memories, because 'the past not only changed, but changed continuously', which Winston finds 'more terrifying than mere torture and death'. There is an emphasis on time and clocks, but there is some uncertainty about what time it really is. This, no doubt, is another Party strategy designed to maintain supreme control.

Winston can remember few concrete details of the past. He is sure that London cannot always have been so 'bleak', 'rundown' and 'depressed', but has trouble extracting a childhood memory to confirm this. To help your study of this element of the text, research pictures and descriptions of the effects of the Blitz on post-war London. Sometimes the past is evoked for Winston through the senses of smell and taste. The aroma of roasting coffee takes him back for an instant to 'the half-forgotten world of his childhood'. Although he cannot get the old man in the prole pub to state that things used to be better, the past is usually presented as in every way preferable to the current state of Oceania. One way in which this is done is through prized objects, like the beautiful notebook Winston uses as a diary, with its sensual 'smooth creamy paper', the engraving of the church, and the paperweight, which has an air of 'belonging to an age quite different from the present one'. When it is smashed by the Thought Police it represents a further destruction of the past.

Charrington's room, in which Winston feels secure, awakens 'a sort of nostalgia, a sort of ancestral memory' in him and is described as 'a pocket of the past'. The past represents safety, even though his childhood was unsettled, being a time of war and hunger when all his close relations disappeared. Through a dream of his mother, Winston realises that the fundamental difference between the past and the present is that in the past there was 'privacy, love and friendship' and people stood by each other, whereas now the predominant emotions are 'fear, hatred and pain'.

The newspaper clipping of Jones, Aaronson and Rutherford is the only concrete evidence Winston has had that the past has been altered. He now sees it as significant enough 'to blow the Party to atoms' (a veiled warning of atomic war?), but he consigned it to the flames of the memory hole. He is 'afflicted with the sense of nightmare' because he cannot understand why, in the long term, the Party practises this deception. The past obsesses him, but by the last chapter he has been brainwashed to deny it, and dismisses his recollection of a happy moment playing with his mother as a 'false memory'. It seems that now there is no one left to care about the preservation of truth, apart from the reader.

Propaganda

Propaganda is information, especially of a biased or misleading nature, that is used to promote or publicise a particular political cause or point of view.

The setting of *Nineteen Eighty-Four* is one filled with propaganda, from the ubiquitous posters of Big Brother to the re-written history books. It is used in obvious and also subtle ways. The Two Minutes Hate, for example, is a blatant way of denouncing enemies of the State and encouraging the people to direct their anger and hatred at a common target. The parading of beaten Eurasian prisoners through Victory Square, however, is a more subtle way of achieving the same ends – patriotic devotion to the Party. Propaganda is a vital tool, and there is an entire workplace devoted to it, ironically titled the Ministry of Truth. Winston spends every day taking factual information and changing it so that certain individuals are denounced, while Big Brother's achievements are exalted. There is no escape, even during lunch breaks, for the air is constantly filled with the biased 'noise-pollution', regaling the latest economic and political successes. One of the key functions of the telescreens is to perpetuate propaganda.

Rats

> *Of all the horrors in the world – a rat!*

Rats, symbol of Winston's underlying fear and his final undoing, lurk just out of clear sight for the reader until they make a dramatic appearance in Room 101 in Part III. In Part I there is a hint that they are always near the surface in Winston's thoughts; he observes that the doorways in the prole district, which open straight onto the pavement, are 'curiously suggestive of rat-holes'. Neither Winston nor the reader sees the rat when it appears in Part II in Charrington's room, only being made aware by Julia's sudden action of hurling a shoe at it. Her very matter-of-fact attitude about infestations of rats and their attacks on children, highlights Winston's debilitating fear, his 'black instant of panic'. He recollects a recurring nightmare, in which 'something unendurable, something too dreadful to be faced' lies behind a wall of darkness. He realises that he knows that the thing is linked with what Julia says about the 'nasty' behaviour of rats, but he cannot yet face up to it.

This self-deception applies to many aspects of his life. Winston knows that terror awaits him in the Ministry of Love, though he brings down the shutters and will not acknowledge what form this terror will take, in the same way that he has 'his eyes tightly shut' when Julia talks about rats in the bedroom. Significantly, the rat appears from the skirting board immediately below the picture, which in turn is connected to the nursery rhyme with the ominous last lines. This emphasises how fragile their sanctuary is; particularly when we realise that the telescreen, which has monitored the whole incident, is hidden behind the picture.

In the film version of the novel, starring John Hurt and made in 1984, rats feature in Winston's dreams of the past, including a nightmare of them running over his mother's dead body. Watch the film to help with your study of this element of the novel.

Just before the rat appears, as if on cue, Winston is thinking about the horror contained in the Ministry of Love: 'There it lay, fixed in future time, preceding death as surely as 99 preceded 100.' What he leaves unsaid, because he has not yet heard of the place, is that 100 precedes 101 – the room of unspeakable horrors, which must precede death, and may even cause it.

At the beginning of Part III, when Winston is in prison, he feels a 'gnawing' hunger. This may be a familiar metaphorical expression, but it still contains a suggestion of rodents, in preparation for Room 101. When he is at last put in there, he has to face the fact that rats were always behind the wall in his dreams. Now the rats come into full view, being gradually moved closer to him, so that he can see clear details of their 'blunt', 'fierce' faces. These are fully grown, enormous rats; one is 'an old scaly grandfather of the sewers'. Orwell relies on the senses of sight, touch, smell, sound and taste to convey the full horror of the rats. Winston at last realises that the only way to save himself from being eaten alive is to transfer the torture to Julia, in other words complete betrayal of her.

Orwell's own strong fear of rats must have helped him to write convincingly about Winston's terror.

Rhymes and songs

Rhymes and songs are used frequently throughout the novel, gaining in importance for Winston and for the reader, who should be aware that any pattern or repetition is significant in a work of fiction. There are three main rhymes and songs: the nursery rhyme 'Oranges and Lemons'; 'The Chestnut Tree', associated with the café; and the popular song 'It was only a hopeless fancy', warbled by the prole woman while hanging up her washing.

By giving the words of the songs, Orwell signals their importance. Mr Charrington introduces 'Oranges and Lemons' when Winston takes an interest in the picture of the church of St Clement Dane in The Strand. He claims not to know the whole rhyme, thereby exciting Winston's curiosity, but does divulge the beginning and the end. This is Charrington's way of prompting Winston, something which he does later when he mentions other rhymes (of which, again, he only seems to know tempting sections). The concept of 'not knowing the middle' links to Winston's perception of his life — he knows that he will end up in the Ministry of Love, preparing for his death, but he does not know the intervening steps. Appropriately it is O'Brien who supplies the missing lines, for he is the one who controls Winston's actions. The rhyme is last used, in a rather theatrical way, when Charrington throws Winston the lines, 'Here comes a candle to light you to bed, here comes a chopper to chop off your head!' just before the Thought Police crash into the room.

The rhyme and the picture link to the theme of the past. The rhyme intrigues Winston: 'It was curious, but when you said it to yourself you had the illusion of actually hearing bells, the bells of a lost London that still existed somewhere or other.' In this instance, the bells are seen as a sign of hope, but they are used in other, contrasting ways elsewhere in the novel. In the same chapter, Winston remembers some of the Party slogans 'like a leaden knell'. A 'knell' is a death bell. Julia and Winston meet in a glade of bluebells for their first love making, then in a disused belfry. What significance do you think Orwell intended?

There are also songs written especially for the population. There is the Hate Song, which we do not hear, written as the theme song for Hate Week, and 'It was only a hopeless fancy', a computer-generated song designed to appeal to the proles. This is sung on every appearance of the fat, prole grandmother. Although the narrator is dismissive about this song, describing it as 'dreadful rubbish', its words have some significance to Winston's position. In the two short verses we have many of the key ideas and events of the novel: the 'hopeless fancy' (Winston's rebellion); the 'April Day' (when the novel begins and Winston starts his diary); 'the dreams they stirred' (Winston's many dreams, nightmares and visions); 'the smiles and the tears across the years' (the importance of the past). The spontaneous singing of this woman echoes that of the thrush and is the last thing that Winston and Julia hear before they are arrested. It is this singing, in the face of a hard existence, that reinforces Winston's belief: 'If there was hope, it lay in the proles.' Could this woman be one of the 'props' set up by the Thought Police? After all, she does appear, like clockwork, every time Winston looks out of the window.

The song 'The Chestnut Tree' is linked with The Chestnut Tree Café and with death and betrayal, for this is the place frequented by the 'traitors' Jones, Aaronson and Rutherford before they are vaporized, and where Winston spends most of his days, while awaiting 'the bullet in the back of the neck'. The original song on which Orwell based it was popular in the 1940s, so contemporary readers would have been very aware of the changes that he made. The original is a charming love song, based on a poem about a blacksmith. The song Winston hears turns the idyllic setting of the protective tree into a place of betrayal:

'Underneath the spreading chestnut tree I sold you and you sold me –'

The use of 'sold' in this context emphasises the sordid aspect of the dealings, as if anything can be got for money. Winston first hears the song on a visit to the café, before he has had any contact with Julia, so the words are prophetic. In the third line, 'There lie they, and here lie we', the verb 'lie' suggests both love and deception.

Dreams

Winston's many dreams are sometimes in the form of reliving or reinterpreting past events, and sometimes a view of the future. The novel is full of the semantics of dreams – 'nightmare', 'reverie', 'daydream', 'vision' and 'hallucination' are used as alternative words. Orwell was interested in his own dreams, which he analysed, and he even had some accurate visions of future events. For this reason, it is fair to pay some attention to the importance of Winston's dreams. His tendency to dream is an indication of his troubled, introspective nature. By contrast, it is unlikely that the unimaginative Parsons was really revealed as a traitor by talking in his sleep. He was clearly set up by his vile children.

Seven years before the novel starts, Winston has a dream in which O'Brien says: 'We shall meet in the place where there is no darkness.' This statement acquires significance as the years pass. Winston knows it will come about, but does not understand the horrific implications of the reference. Other dreams foretell specific events, such as the one of Julia in the Golden Country, but sometimes they throw light on past events and his relationship with his mother. Dreams also show that nothing is sacred in this society. Even dreams can be violated, for O'Brien seems to have intercepted Winston's and knows all about them. A dream ultimately leads Winston to Room 101, when he cries out Julia's name in his sleep, showing that his love is still for her rather than for Big Brother.

The paperweight

Winston first sees the paperweight in Mr Charrington's shop in Chapter VIII. He is instantly attracted to it and it is described using beautiful, natural imagery. The glass itself looks like 'rain-water' and it contains coral, which looks like 'a rose or a sea anemone'. Significantly, the coral lies at its 'heart', suggesting it is a precious, living thing, surrounded by the debris of death and war. Winston likes the fact that it has little purpose other than as decoration, as such things have long since been eradicated by the Party.

The paperweight later takes on greater significance when Winston imagines that it is a symbol of his clandestine, private life with Julia. The fact that the ornament itself is secret makes this even more appropriate. After making love with Julia, Winston examines the glass and is fascinated by the depth of the interior, which is 'transparent as air'. He describes it as 'sky' coloured and calls it a 'tiny world with its atmosphere complete'. This also reveals how he feels about his relationship with Julia. Alone in their rented room, with luxury foods and the time to talk about non-Party matters, Winston feels that they have created their own, perfect microcosm. The coral at the centre, he feels, symbolises 'Julia's life and his own'. He again refers to the 'heart of the crystal', enforcing the idea that this is a living object. Certainly, it seems to exert some appeal over both characters – even Julia brings it to the bed to have a look at it 'in better light'.

Considering the significance of the paperweight, it is a terrible moment when it is 'smashed to pieces' by one of the police thugs who come to arrest Julia and Winston. Once shattered, Orwell describes the coral as 'a tiny crinkle of pink' like 'a sugar rosebud from a cake'. These similes are delicate and redolent of a baby's fragility or the decoration on a wedding cake, thus even more heartbreaking that they should be destroyed. Winston also notices how 'small' the coral is inside the glass. This shows that compared with the Party, the lives and ideals of Winston and Julia are tiny and unimportant.

After their arrest, Charrington orders one of the police to 'pick up those pieces', once he spots them on the floor. This is an unusual request and we wonder why he has any interest in them at all. Does he have a yearning for the object himself or, more likely as the coral represents Winston and Julia, does this suggest that they are truly in the hands of the Thought Police, and that Charrington is not prepared to discard them, just yet?

Text commentary

Part I – Chapters I to VIII

Chapter I

> **"The clocks were striking thirteen"**

The opening chapter begins in April 1984. Life is <u>bleak</u> in Oceania – there is <u>no</u> <u>privacy,</u> <u>no</u> <u>pleasure</u> and every activity is prescribed. Posters of Big Brother are visible everywhere. A <u>science</u> <u>fiction</u> note is created immediately by the clock. Our initial impression is that this is an <u>alien</u> <u>world</u>, where even time works differently, and the negative connotations of <u>thirteen</u> are significant. However, we later find out that this system is not so very different, just a twenty-four hour clock.

It rapidly becomes apparent that Winston Smith does not live in an age of sophisticated mechanisation accessible to all. While the authorities have technology in the form of telescreens to control the population, the people themselves live a <u>poor,</u> <u>depressing</u> <u>existence</u>, with lifts that don't work, rubbish strewing the streets and run-down housing. The opening emphasises the <u>cheerless</u> <u>atmosphere</u> and sets a <u>sombre</u> <u>tone</u> for the book with adjectives such as 'cold', 'vile', 'gritty' and 'torn'. Life is not comfortable.

Explore

Why do you think Orwell chose these names in particular for the Ministries? What connotations do they have?

We learn about the political structure and the primary government departments: the <u>Ministry</u> <u>of</u> <u>Truth</u>, concerned with news, entertainment and education; the <u>Ministry</u> <u>of</u> <u>Peace</u>, concerned with war; the <u>Ministry</u> <u>of</u> <u>Love</u>, maintaining law and order; and the <u>Ministry</u> <u>of</u> <u>Plenty</u>, which controls economic affairs.

The names are significant and indicate that nothing is as it seems in this world; nothing should be taken at face value, either by us or by Winston.

❝ *The world looked cold* ❞

Winston Smith returns to his flat in Victory Mansions for his lunch break from the Ministry of Truth. The run-down block is dominated by posters of the face of the political leader, the Stalin-like <u>Big Brother</u>.

Explore

Explore the use of media in the novel. What parallels are there between the modern Channel 4 show 'Big Brother' and the world of *Nineteen Eighty-Four*?

Inside the flat the <u>telescreen</u> is on, watching and listening to his every move, but because of its position in the room, Winston is able to sit undetected in an <u>alcove</u>. As a character Winston is not made to seem attractive – his body is meagre, his skin rough and he suffers from a varicose ulcer on his leg. Do you think this sore might have deeper significance? In contrast, Big Brother is dark, robust and '<u>ruggedly</u> <u>handsome</u>'.

In his room Winston begins writing a <u>diary</u>, an activity which could be punishable by death. He knows he could be arrested for '<u>thoughtcrime</u>', even if he destroys what he has written, but he has been motivated by a shared look with an Inner Party member, O'Brien, during that morning's <u>Two</u> <u>Minutes</u> <u>Hate</u> – a time during which the workers are incited to denounce Emmanuel Goldstein, who has stood up to Big Brother and is seen as the main enemy of the people. We are also introduced to a young woman, Julia, who makes him feel uneasy. Winston notes that he feels a '<u>peculiar</u> <u>uneasiness</u>' whenever he is near her and fails to realise that this is a strong <u>sexual</u> <u>attraction</u>. Why do you think this might make him so <u>uncomfortable</u>?

A knock at the door surprises him, but he must answer it straight away, because it would cause suspicion if he hesitated.

Chapter II

> **"Up with your hands!"** *yelled a savage voice*

Mrs <u>Parsons</u>, a neighbour, calls on Winston to ask if he will look at her sink, which he successfully unblocks. The visit to her flat gives Orwell the opportunity to show in more detail the appalling conditions in which people live and also, far more alarmingly, the role of <u>children</u> in society. At first the Parsons children are just a noise in another room, but gradually the full picture of their <u>violent</u> and <u>vindictive</u> nature emerges. The boy and girl, both under ten, are keen members of the <u>Spies</u>, a far cry from the Scouting movement, despite the team spirit, parades and hikes, and closer to the <u>Hitler Youth</u>. This mother is frightened of her children, who are more likely to denounce her to the Thought Police than to play with their toys.

Explore

The Hitler Youth was organised in 1933, to prepare the young for further military action. Motto: 'Be violent and dominating'. Does this remind you of the Parsons children?

They are being particularly difficult this afternoon, because they are missing the hanging of some Eurasian prisoners. As Winston leaves, the boy hits him in the neck with a catapult and calls him 'Goldstein' – in effect calling him a traitor.

Explore

What details does Orwell include to make these children so disturbing?

When Winston returns to his diary, he remembers a <u>dream</u> he had 7 years ago in which a voice, later identified as O'Brien's, said to him: '<u>We shall meet in the place where there is no darkness</u>.' This mysterious phrase returns to haunt him and is not explained until the third part of the novel. The <u>lack of communication</u> in this society, and Winston's need for it, is shown by his empathy with O'Brien, whether he is a friend or an enemy. The telescreen announces that there has been a victory in India, and follows this with the news that the chocolate ration is to be reduced.

Explore

Research 'rationing'. Chocolate was still rationed after World War Two when Orwell was writing *Nineteen Eighty-Four*.

What does this indicate about the strategies of the Party? Winston attempts to hide his diary before leaving for work.

Chapter III

<u>Dreams</u> feature significantly in this chapter. They are a device used by Orwell to give information on Winston's <u>past</u>, while showing his turmoil in the <u>present</u>. His first dream features his <u>mother and sister</u>, both now dead, whose lives have been sacrificed to save his own. The next dream episode takes place in Winston's regular dream landscape, <u>the Golden Country</u>, and involves Julia. Do you think there is any significance in Winston waking up saying Shakespeare's name?

> **❝You can do better than that. You're not trying❞**

Explore

Research 'P.T', a form of parade-ground exercise. Can you think of other examples of communal physical training?

While Winston takes part in the <u>Physical Jerks</u> on the <u>telescreen</u> he tries to recollect his childhood and compare it with the present. This enables Orwell to give the reader necessary background on the changes in the world map, the war, doublethink, Big Brother and Ingsoc. Winston is personally reprimanded by the female instructor when he does not try hard enough with his exercises, which proves just how closely he is being <u>monitored</u>.

Chapter IV

> **❝Day by day and almost minute by minute the past was brought up to date❞**

We see Winston's working routine in the Records Department of the Ministry of Truth. His job is to '<u>rectify</u>' news items. This '<u>putting right</u>' means altering the information to suit the needs of the Party. Newspapers and all media are changed if there is the slightest political significance to the content. Winston thinks about his fellow workers and the workings of the Ministry, whose main function is to supply the people of

Oceania with 'every conceivable kind of information, instruction or entertainment'.

Explore

Research purges in Stalinist Russia and modern South America.

Despite knowing that what he is doing is meaningless and untruthful, Winston works efficiently and takes satisfaction in the more difficult assignments, which test him intellectually. His most challenging job is rewriting an Order of the Day from Big Brother to remove reference to Comrade Withers, an 'unperson'. Winston informs us of the number of people who disappear, and how all trace of them ever having existed is obliterated. Does this information make us concerned for Winston's future safety?

Winston has no moral scruples in inventing a heroic figure, Comrade Ogilvy, to take the place of Withers. He becomes fully involved in his fiction, which he feels will meet the full approval of his superiors. It is easy for him to adopt the voice of Big Brother in his work, showing how much of an influence this figurehead has had.

Chapter V

> 66*There will be no thought as we understand it now* 99

Explore

Why is Newspeak so important to Big Brother? Visit www.newspeakdictionary.com

Winston lunches in the canteen at the Ministry of Truth and chats to his comrade, Syme, an expert in Newspeak, who is working on the new dictionary. They discuss rationing before collecting their miserable lunch. Winston suddenly realises that Syme is so intelligent he is destined to be 'vaporized', as he explains how the language is to be pared down until everyone speaks the same, unemotional, objective language, created by Big Brother.

> 66*Fabulous statistics* 99

Parsons appears and tells them how his daughter trailed a strange man and handed him over to the Patrols because he was wearing 'a funny kind of shoes'. He is proud of his children's zealous passion for the Spies and, unlike Winston, does not appear to realise how lethal they might prove to be. An announcement details the wealth of the State and spews out false records of productivity and economic success. It is ironic that while the government pretends the times are prosperous, ordinary people are surviving on the most meagre of supplies, without complaint. Instead of looking like the healthy 'blonde-haired, vital' youths set up by the Party as ideal, they are haggard-looking, 'dark and ill-favoured'.

Explore

Find out about Hitler's ideas on the 'Aryan Race'. Are there any similarities?

Winston notices the girl with the dark hair and feels a sense of panic and paranoia, wondering whether he is guilty of 'facecrime' (wearing an inappropriate expression on your face). The whistle signals the return to work.

Chapter VI

Winston writes his diary, struggling with his emotions as he recalls a time in the past when he was driven to use an old, toothless prostitute. He was married at the time, but his loneliness, frustration and craving for some kind of emotional connection was so great that he took this enormous risk, even though the penalty might be 5 years in a Labour camp.

> **Sexual intercourse was to be looked on as a slightly disgusting minor operation**

The memory reminds him of Katharine his tall, fair-haired wife, selected for him by the Party. He explains that Big Brother has no desire to see men and women happily in love, because then they would be harder to control. Instead, the Party's aim is to remove all pleasure from any sexual relationship, and children are indoctrinated with this belief from an early age. Katharine was a loyal Party member, and Winston found their active, but <u>cold, loveless marriage</u> unbearable. They eventually parted when Katharine failed to become pregnant. The chapter ends with Winston wanting to scream out to vent some of his frustrations.

Chapter VII

Winston believes that hope for the future lies with the <u>proles</u>, the mass of the population, but he notes resignedly that they have no interest in <u>rebellion</u>.

> *How could you tell how much of it was lies?*

Winston recalls a history textbook, filled with <u>nonsense and blatant propaganda</u>. Reading it makes him remember one enlightening moment, when he first finds <u>concrete evidence that history is being changed</u>. After Goldstein flees, Winston spots three of his followers, Jones, Aaronson and Rutherford, drinking in the Chestnut Tree Café. Ironically, the telescreen is playing a song: '<u>Under the spreading chestnut tree/ I sold you and you sold me</u>.' He remembers later finding an old newspaper article, reporting that the three men had been rearrested and detailing when they had confessed to crimes against the State. Winston notices that the dates do not tally, so he knows this information must be false. He does not understand the significance of this memory, but is shocked to have found tangible evidence of <u>past-doctoring</u>. He disposes of the newspaper article and considers this incident. Winston finds courage by thinking about O'Brien and decides to continue writing the diary for him.

Chapter VIII

After missing a second meeting at the Community Centre, Winston ponders 'ownlife', a frowned-upon <u>sense of individuality</u> that often marks Party members as dangerous.

As he is searching for a personal sense of 'ownlife', Winston finds himself drawn to the 'brown-coloured' <u>slums</u>. He notices the 'puddles of filthy water' and the windows, 'broken and boarded up'. The description is filled with images of <u>decay</u> <u>and</u> <u>ruin</u> and symbols of a shattered way of life. In a literal representation of this, a bomb falls over the city, covering Winston with fragments of glass, a recurring motif in this chapter. As Winston recovers he notices the stump of an arm and kicks the '<u>thing</u>' into the gutter. His use of the word 'thing', perhaps indicates his <u>de-sensitivisation</u> at the hands of the Party.

❝Were things better than they are now, or were they worse?❞

Wandering through the slums, he spots a pub and enters to ask one of the older <u>proles</u> what he can remember about <u>life</u> <u>before</u> <u>the War</u>. Winston buys an old man a drink and gently questions him about his past. Interested only in the minutiae of life, the man fondly remembers days when he drank pints, not litres, and recalls a world of lackeys, flunkies and 'parasites'. It is worth noting that his memories are not dissimilar from the world they currently inhabit, with a privileged ruling class and a subordinate under class. Winston is frustrated and compares the proles to <u>ants</u>, who can see '<u>small</u> <u>objects</u> <u>but</u> <u>not</u> <u>large</u> <u>ones</u>'. This is a significant simile, considering that an ant colony can achieve enormous feats thanks to combined strength and sheer numbers. Winston is wrong to feel so disheartened.

❝His feet had brought him back here of their own accord❞

As if to seek comfort, Winston finds himself at the <u>junk</u> <u>shop</u> and is warmly welcomed. In a <u>mirror</u> <u>of</u> <u>the</u> <u>outside</u> <u>world</u>, the contents are largely 'broken up' or 'melted down'. Despite the 'litter' of the discarded and the useless, Winston spots 'a heavy lump of glass, curved on one side, flat on the other, making almost a hemisphere'. Orwell uses natural imagery to describe the <u>paperweight</u>, enhancing its beauty, and Winston does not hesitate to buy it, to Mr Charrington's delight.

> **❝** *Here comes a candle to light you to bed,*
> *Here comes a chopper to chop off*
> *your head* **❞**

Sensing his interest, Charrington shows Winston a room upstairs, which contains an enormous bed and is warm and inviting. Almost psychically picking up on Winston's nostalgic mood, Charrington recites '<u>Oranges</u> <u>and</u> <u>Lemons</u>' after showing Winston a picture of a church on the wall. He cannot remember the whole poem, but ominously recalls the last lines.

> **❝** *The girl was spying on him* **❞**

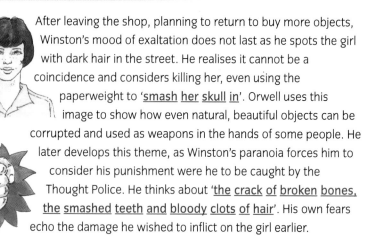

After leaving the shop, planning to return to buy more objects, Winston's mood of exaltation does not last as he spots the girl with dark hair in the street. He realises it cannot be a coincidence and considers killing her, even using the paperweight to '<u>smash</u> <u>her</u> <u>skull</u> <u>in</u>'. Orwell uses this image to show how even natural, beautiful objects can be corrupted and used as weapons in the hands of some people. He later develops this theme, as Winston's paranoia forces him to consider his punishment were he to be caught by the Thought Police. He thinks about '<u>the</u> <u>crack</u> <u>of</u> <u>broken</u> <u>bones,</u> <u>the</u> <u>smashed</u> <u>teeth</u> <u>and</u> <u>bloody</u> <u>clots</u> <u>of</u> <u>hair</u>'. His own fears echo the damage he wished to inflict on the girl earlier.

> **We shall meet in the place where there is no darkness**

Winston thinks about O'Brien's words and suddenly realises that this place is the imagined future, which everyone could believe in. Unable to concentrate on this, however, he visualises the face of Big Brother and remembers the oxymoronic slogans: '<u>WAR</u> <u>IS</u> <u>PEACE,</u> <u>FREEDOM</u> <u>IS</u> <u>SLAVERY,</u> <u>IGNORANCE</u> <u>IS</u> <u>STRENGTH</u>'. Part I concludes in this sombre mood, made more 'leaden' after Winston's tantalising glimpse of hope and optimism.

Quick questions

1   *In which month does the novel start?*

2   *Who is featured on the posters everywhere?*

3   *What does Winston start to write?*

4   *Why does Winston visit the Parsons' flat?*

5   *Who calls Winston a spy and threatens to vaporize him?*

6   *What is the name of Winston's colleague, the Newspeak specialist?*

7   *Who does Winston suspect is watching and following him?*

8   *Who is Katharine?*

9   *What are 'steamers' in the prole district?*

10   *What does Winston buy from the junk-shop?*

A process of elimination

1   *London is the main city of Airforce One/Airstrip One/Airbase One.*

2   *Winston works in the Ministry of Truth/Love/Peace.*

3   *Winston catches Julia's/O'Brien's/Parsons' eye in the Two Minutes Hate.*

4   *Winston thinks Parsons/Mrs Parsons/Julia will be vaporized.*

5   *O'Brien/Charrington/Old prole man first mentions Oranges and Lemons.*

Complete the quotations

1   *'The clocks were striking _____.'*

2   *'If there is hope, it lies in the _____'. Who says this?*

3   *'War is _____.' (Party slogan)*

4   *'Freedom is the freedom to say that two plus two make _____.' (diary entry)*

5   *'Here comes a chopper to _____.'*

Impressions of Winston

1   *What is Winston's attitude to women?*

2   *What is Winston's attitude to his work?*

3   *How do we learn about Winston's childhood?*

4   *Why is Winston drawn to O'Brien?*

5   *Why does Winston find Charrington's upstairs room so appealing?*

Who is this?

1   *'a smallish, frail figure, the meagreness of his body merely emphasised by the blue overall'*

2   *'a large, burly man with a thick neck and a coarse, humorous, brutal face'*

3   *'a man of about forty-five, with a heavy black moustache and ruggedly handsome features'*

4   *'a lean Jewish face, with a great fuzzy aureole of white hair and a small goatee beard'*

5   *'a tubby, middle-sized man with fair hair and a frog-like face'*

6   *'a bold-looking girl of about twenty-seven, with thick dark hair, a freckled face and swift, athletic movements'*

7   *'a colourless, crushed-looking woman, with wispy hair and a lined face'*

8   *'a tall, fair-haired girl, very straight, with splendid movements'*

9   *'a man of perhaps sixty, frail and bowed, with a long, benevolent nose'*

10 *'a handsome, tough-looking boy of nine'*

Text commentary

Part II – Chapters I to X

Chapter I

> **❝*I love you*❞**

At work Winston sees the <u>mysterious girl</u> with her arm in a sling. He instinctively helps her as she falls, and as he does so, she slips him a <u>personal note</u>. Winston is '<u>stunned</u>' and spends several days trying to engineer an opportunity to talk with her – something <u>forbidden</u> under Party rules. The note throws him into <u>confusion</u>, expressed with images suggesting <u>anxiety</u>: 'like a restless dream', 'as though a fire were burning in his belly'. The girl has the power to <u>disrupt</u> his peace of mind and fill him with <u>dangerous emotions</u>. Over a week later, they snatch a quick conversation in the canteen. A meeting is arranged by the girl: Nineteen Hours, Victory Square.

> **❝*Instead of the eyes of the girl, the eyes of the aged prisoner gazed mournfully at Winston*❞**

Explore

Where does the word 'proletarian' come from? What does it mean?

The first meeting is tense and Winston despairs of being able to talk with the girl, as his way is hampered by crowds of proles. Eventually, he manages to stand next to the girl, watching a convoy of trucks carrying <u>Eurasian prisoners</u> pass. The girl gives Winston directions to meet her on Sunday in a clearing in a wood, far away from the city.

Despite the danger and the fact that Winston cannot look at Julia directly, the moment is <u>sensuous</u>, with imagery focused on touch; verbs such as '<u>pressed</u>', '<u>feel</u>' and '<u>clasped</u>' are used. Winston appears <u>sensitive</u> as he grasps the girl's hand,

intricately exploring its shape. The moment is <u>erotic</u> because it is such a small gesture, but <u>personal, secret and forbidden</u>, and stolen against a contrasting backdrop of war, torture and military activity – an ominous reminder of Winston's fate, should they be caught in their illicit affair.

Chapter II

> ❝*The ground was misty with bluebells* ❞

Explore

Pathetic fallacy: when nature and weather echo an emotion.

Winston travels to the chosen meeting place, in a chapter filled with <u>romantic, natural imagery</u>. Using pathetic fallacy, Orwell describes a scene of <u>Spring idyll</u>. The language is <u>tender</u>, with connotations of <u>love</u> and even hints of the <u>marriage</u> ceremony: 'pools of gold', 'ring-doves', 'kiss one's skin'.

Winston arrives early and begins to pick a large bunch of <u>bluebells</u> with the intention of presenting them as a romantic gift to Julia. When she appears he becomes <u>paranoid and insecure</u>, imagining that in full sunlight she will be repulsed by the way he looks. They talk and embrace, but Winston initially feels too tense and frightened by her passion to reciprocate: 'it was too soon, her youth and prettiness had frightened him'.

> ❝*For whom, for what, was that bird singing?* ❞

They talk about life in the Party and Julia reveals much about her character, after giving Winston a piece of black market <u>chocolate</u> – a real luxury. They walk through the woods, relaxed but still careful to keep out of sight. Winston recalls the '<u>Golden Country</u>' dreams, a landscape redolent of the '<u>Golden Age</u>' (an illusionary time of plenty, wealth and peace). Suddenly and poetically a <u>song thrush</u> begins singing:

'a torrent of song'. After the silence, it seems as though the creature sings to rejoice in their new relationship. Winston, feeling <u>uplifted</u> <u>and</u> <u>passionate</u>, leads Julia back into the clearing and they make love and then doze in the dappled shade. Julia admits that she has done this many times, but Winston loves her all the more for this admission. He sees their relationship as much as a <u>political</u> <u>act</u> <u>of</u> <u>defiance</u> as a romantic liaison, and believes they have struck a blow against Big Brother.

Explore

Read Thomas Hardy's poem 'The Darkling Thrush' in relation to this passage.

Chapter III

After waking up Julia is '<u>businesslike</u>' and gives Winston directions to get home safely. She tells Winston where they might meet the following week. After kissing him '<u>violently</u>' she leaves. The following month they are able to meet only once in the '<u>belfry</u> <u>of</u> <u>a</u> <u>ruinous</u> <u>church</u>'. The fact that such a symbol of <u>holiness</u> and <u>spirituality</u> should be in tatters, indicates that there is no room for this kind of religious belief in this society.

Explore

Karl Marx said: 'Religion is the opium of the people.' What do you think he meant by this?

When the two characters next meet a rocket <u>bomb</u> explodes and, although neither of them is harmed, Julia is thrown to the ground and covered in plaster dust. She looks like a <u>corpse</u> and Winston fears that she may have been killed. Their meetings are filled with this kind of ominous reminder that their relationship is ultimately <u>doomed</u>. Julia reveals more of her background – the fact that she appears to be a model citizen and industrious member of the Anti-Sex League while leading such a vigorous and convincing <u>double</u> <u>life</u> gives us an insight into this society. How many other hypocrisies are taking place at even higher levels?

> ❝The clever thing was to break the rules and stay alive❞

Winston confides in her about his wife and Julia expounds violently on the Party's motivation for making sex distasteful, explaining that it makes people divert their energies instead into Big Brother, Three Year Plans and the Two Minutes Hate.

 Winston recalls an occasion when he and Katharine took part in a <u>community hike</u> and got separated from the others. Winston, observant of all things natural, pointed out an unusual flower to his wife: 'One tuft was of two colours, magenta and brick-red, apparently growing on the same root.' (Winston does not realise the significance of such a discovery – what he is seeing is <u>nature's ability to break the rules</u>, in the same way that Winston will later. In the natural order of society, Winston is the single, brightly-coloured, mutant bloom.) Katharine was not interested and it occured to Winston that it would be very simple to push her off the cliff-top and end his miserable marriage. Julia wonders why he did not but Winston explains that it would not have made any difference.

> **❝In this game that we're playing, we can't win❞**

Winston explains that he is a realist, but compared with Julia he has a pessimistic outlook. He confesses his fear of dying, while knowing the inevitability of it. Julia, however, does not accept this view and, in a more positive act, begins to draw a map detailing their next meeting.

Chapter IV

Winston and Julia meet again in a room Winston has hired above Mr Charrington's shop. Outside, a <u>prole woman</u> is singing a <u>popular song</u> which, in its own way, is poignant. She talks of a love affair and 'dreams they stirred'. It is a sentimental ballad that, like the thrush's song, seems curiously appropriate.

Winston risks hiring the room because he is becoming frustrated at the lack of opportunities to get together with Julia and he wants them to become closer, more than just rebels against Big Brother. Orwell repeats the phrase '<u>He wished</u>' three times to emphasise how far from Winston's dreams of a real relationship their current situation is.

> **❝❝ *I'm going to be a woman, not a Party Comrade* ❞❞**

Julia arrives at the room with a stash of stolen, <u>black market</u>, luxury items: sugar, coffee, bread, jam and tea. She asks Winston to turn away, and when he is allowed to look she has painted her face and is wearing perfume. He notices that it is the same scent the <u>prostitute</u> wore and this heightens Julia's presence as a <u>real woman</u> and a sexual being. Later, when Winston wakes up, he finds some of her <u>make-up</u> has smudged onto his own face – they are literally becoming closer. Winston is made happy by Julia's personality 'rubbing off' onto him.

> **❝❝ *Of all the horrors in the world – a rat!* ❞❞**

While talking, Julia suddenly spots a <u>rat</u> and hurls a shoe at it. Winston is startled and remembers a vivid <u>nightmare</u>, a '<u>wall of darkness</u>'. Orwell uses <u>violent language</u> to express the depth of Winston's fear, with adjectives such as 'unendurable', 'dreadful' and 'deadly'. In a way, the darkness is representative of the world of Big Brother. Winston knows, on a certain level, that it is a nightmarish, unseen threat, but he cannot see where the danger is, and only subconsciously feels its presence.

> **❝❝ *A tiny world with its atmosphere complete* ❞❞**

Julia notices the <u>picture</u> of St Clement Dane Church and to Winston's surprise is able to recall the next line of the rhyme.

Like Mr Charrington earlier, she ominously recalls <u>the ending</u>. It seems that everyone can remember the final warning. In another ironic touch she wonders whether the picture has '<u>bugs behind it</u>'. It certainly has, but not in the way Julia suspects! The chapter ends with Winston looking at the paperweight and imagining that it is symbolic of his life with Julia.

Chapter V

<u>Syme</u> has disappeared, as surely as Winston predicted, despite his obvious value to the Party. Orwell concentrates on the frenetic preparations for <u>Hate Week</u> and uses listing to build up a picture of intense activity, although the industrious actions are always tainted with sinister overtones. Orwell informs us that in addition to songs and slogans being learned, '<u>rumours</u>' are circulated and '<u>photographs are faked</u>'. This reminds us that all these activities, which parallel the celebrations that were held for D-Day or VE Day, are much more menacing. After all, the sole purpose is to generate a <u>patriotic frenzy</u> of 'hate' towards the Party's enemies. These preparations take place against a background of <u>rocket bomb explosions and violent deaths</u>. Parsons is particularly active, chivvying people and expending enormous amounts of energy in decorating their block of flats.

Explore

Can you think of any patriotic occasions? What ingredients are needed for these events?

Winston and Julia continue to meet, and although the rat is not seen again, the bugs multiply. Orwell, however, describes the room as '<u>paradise</u>', because even though it is squalid and filthy, it is the means for Julia and Winston to experience freedom away from prying eyes and constant monitoring and a place where they feel 'no harm could come to them'.

" It just occurred to me you might be interested "

Charrington continues to fascinate Winston, as he seems to hold the key to the past. He is described as an '<u>extinct</u> <u>animal</u>' and he tempts Winston with small items of stock and snatches of rhymes. It is a pity that Winston does not focus more on the objects he is shown, because in many ways they are distasteful and portentous: 'a scrap of rubbish', a 'broken snuff-box' and 'a strand of some long-dead baby's hair'. In addition, the <u>nursery</u> <u>rhymes</u> contain warnings of their own. 'Cock-Robin', for example, focuses on the suspicious murder of a harmless bird and the song about 'four and-twenty blackbirds' similarly rejoices in small creatures being baked alive. Charrington seems to be slyly toying with Winston, scattering clues about the danger he is in.

Explore

Nursery rhymes are used a lot in *Nineteen Eighty-Four*. Research the words to these rhymes – can you see any significance?

> **❝*You're only a rebel from the waist downwards*❞**

Winston tells Julia about his bond with O'Brien and they discuss rebelling against the Party and finding <u>the</u> <u>Brotherhood</u>, although Julia does not believe Goldstein ever really existed. Expressing suspicions about the rockets and the way the Party uses war for its own ends, Julia shows how <u>intelligent</u> she is, but other than in a personal way she has <u>no</u> <u>interest</u> in questioning the workings of the Party and cannot see the importance of the way history is being deleted and altered.

Chapter VI

Winston is approached by <u>O'Brien</u>, who tells him that he has noticed Winston's flair for using <u>Newspeak</u>, and offers to show him the latest edition of the dictionary. He suggests that Winston visits him at his flat, and gives the address. The fact that O'Brien makes a fleeting reference to Syme, who is now an 'unperson', and shares his address, makes Winston convinced that this is a coded message. The exchange gives him another moment to establish a mutual 'thoughtcrime' with O'Brien. The whole interaction takes place in front of a telescreen, which shows how devious O'Brien is. He acts as if he has nothing to hide.

> **❝ But Syme was not only dead, he was abolished ❞**

Although the conversation begins with a reference to Syme, who has apparently talked to O'Brien about him, Winston is not concerned about his own safety. He does not consider how O'Brien and Syme might have had this conversation, he only worries that O'Brien is putting himself in danger by mentioning an 'unperson'. This reveals a certain trusting, but naïve, nature on Winston's part. He is excited but sees the 'chilly' inevitability of his own death. The fear of this, however, does not outweigh his desire to join the Brotherhood.

Chapter VII

Winston wakes up from an upsetting dream about his mother. Interestingly, the dream appears to take place inside the glass dome of the paperweight – the object that symbolises Winston's private world. He recalls the last time he saw his mother and baby sister.

> **❝ I believed I had murdered my mother ❞**

Thirty years previously, in the rubble and rubbish of a bombed London, Winston remembers how his family were in a state of perpetual starvation with 'fierce, sordid battles at mealtimes'. His father had already disappeared and his mother spent her time trying desperately to feed the remaining family. On one occasion, following a small delivery of chocolate, he begs his mother for more than his share. She willingly gives up her own, but in a moment of greed he also snatches the chocolate from the hand of his dying sister. He runs away and when he returns both his mother and sister have disappeared.

Naturally, this dream is <u>traumatic</u> for Winston – his last family memory is negative; a crying baby and his mother's feeble attempts to pacify her. This image shows how effective the Party already is in dividing family loyalties and creating a fierce, '<u>dog eat dog</u>' battle for survival. Winston literally takes sweets from

the hands of a baby and his dream shows that he has never forgiven himself for this action. This goes some way to explaining why he is so desperately <u>lonely</u> <u>and</u> <u>emotionally</u> <u>stunted</u> at the start of the novel. He concludes that the Party's most effective weapon is to take away people's humanity. Big Brother has effectively replaced 'love' with 'hate', but he realises that <u>humanity</u> is the one quality that <u>the</u> <u>proles</u> have retained, and he respects them for it.

> **❝If they could stop me loving you – that would be the real betrayal ❞**

Julia and Winston discuss what will happen when they are caught and then make a <u>lovers'</u> <u>pact</u>. They know they will be tortured until they confess, but they determine to continue loving each other. As the Thought Police '<u>had</u> <u>never</u> <u>mastered</u> <u>the</u> <u>secret</u> <u>of</u> <u>finding</u> <u>out</u> <u>what</u> <u>another</u> <u>human</u> <u>was</u> <u>thinking</u>', they promise to remain true to their hearts.

Chapter VIII

Winston and Julia visit O'Brien at his flat, and are amazed at the <u>wealth</u> and <u>luxury</u>. Martin, the servant, leads them into O'Brien's office and his attitude makes Winston afraid that he has made a mistake. He is put at ease when O'Brien switches off the telescreen, explaining that this is an Inner Party Member privilege.

After Julia and Winston are given wine, 'a dark-red liquid' which they have never tasted before, Winston talks about the Brotherhood. O'Brien <u>tests</u> him, checking his loyalties by posing a series of questions involving <u>acts of brutality and violence</u>. When O'Brien asks if they are prepared to separate, they reply 'no', although Julia seems more emphatic.

> ❝*A wave of admiration, almost of worship, flowed out from Winston towards O'Brien*❞

O'Brien explains that <u>the Brotherhood</u> exists as a series of individuals working alone, so they cannot implicate each other, should they be caught. He says, '<u>we are the dead</u>', somewhat suspiciously echoing Winston's words in Chapter III. Julia leaves after a final toast. Winston significantly chooses '<u>To the past</u>'. O'Brien arranges to get Winston a copy of '<u>the book</u>'. The chapter ends with O'Brien completing the 'Oranges and Lemons' nursery rhyme. The missing lines are concerned with payment: 'When will you pay me'. Does this have any links to the 'Chestnut Tree' rhyme?

Chapter IX

Winston is exhausted from work, but delights in remembering the word '<u>gelatinous</u>' (jelly-like). While <u>Newspeak</u> prunes language, Winston enjoys expanding his own vocabulary. Preparations for Hate Week continue, but the <u>enemy suddenly switches</u> from Eurasia to Eastasia.

> ❝*The Theory and Practice of Oligarchical Collectivism*❞ *by Emmanual Goldstein*

Winston visits Charrington's room and begins reading the book. The main principles of the text are as follows:

Explore

What does 'collectivism' mean? Can you see the advantages? Has it ever been used, historically?

1. War is economically vital for giving people something to work for. The poor standards of living which result enable the Party to control the masses with ease.

2. People need to believe that Big Brother will be ultimately victorious.

3. Because the war is never-ending, it has stopped having any political importance. All three powers have remained the same, therefore, ironically, 'War is peace'.

4. There have always been three main layers of society: the Upper, the Middle and the Lower, and no action in history has ever increased equality.

5. Wealth is not inherited from person to person, but it is kept within the ruling group.

6. Because Party members are not allowed the slightest deviation of thought, there is a vigorous mental training called 'crimestop', 'blackwhite' and 'doublethink'.

7. The past is defined by records and memories. As the Party controls both of these things, by definition it controls the past.

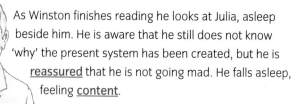

❝He was safe, everything was all right❞

As Winston finishes reading he looks at Julia, asleep beside him. He is aware that he still does not know 'why' the present system has been created, but he is <u>reassured</u> that he is not going mad. He falls asleep, feeling <u>content</u>.

Chapter X

Winston awakes and listens to the words of the <u>prole woman singing</u>. Winston and Julia are filled with a sense of the natural beauty of childbirth and the future, but as they watch the woman, Julia comments prophetically that it 'seems to have got colder'.

> **"***Here comes a chopper to chop off your head***"**

Winston says: '<u>We are the dead</u>', and they are shocked when an <u>'iron' voice</u> repeats these words. Orwell uses repetition throughout the text to highlight key phrases, but here the repetition indicates that although the words might be the same, language can carry different meaning. The picture from the wall smashes onto the ground and they notice the telescreen, which orders them to remain where they are. They realise that they have been <u>discovered</u> and feel <u>terrified</u> when they hear a 'thin, cultivated voice' intone the last line of the nursery rhyme.

The room is suddenly filled with police, one of whom symbolically smashes the paperweight. Their <u>private world</u> is literally <u>shattered</u>. Julia is beaten up and thrown to the floor and Winston watches helplessly as she is carried away. Mr Charrington enters, completely changed in appearance and demeanour. He is a member of the <u>Thought Police</u>.

Quick quiz 2

Quick questions

1   Who does Winston suspect that Julia works for?

2   In which department does Julia work?

3   What black market foodstuff does Julia bring with her to the country?

4   What colour is Julia's Junior Anti-Sex League sash?

5   Who sings: 'It was only an 'opeless fancy'?

6   Who organises the decoration of Victory Mansions for Hate Week?

7   What does O'Brien first offer to lend to Winston?

8   Who is Martin?

9   What is the name of the organisation conspiring against the Party?

10   What colour are the Thought Police uniforms?

A process of elimination

1   Julia gives Winston her note in a corridor/the canteen/Victory Square.

2   Winston and Julia listen to a robin/skylark/thrush singing.

3   Ampleforth/Syme/Parsons disappears.

4   In O'Brien's flat, Winston proposes a toast to the proles/the Brotherhood/the past.

5   Winston reads Goldstein's book at work/in his flat/in Charrington's room.

Complete the quotations

1   'I _____ you' (Julia's note)

2   'Of all the horrors in the world – a ____!' Who says this?

3   'Ignorance is _____.' (Party slogan)

4   'It's the Golden _____.' (Winston)

5   'We are the _____.' (Said on three occasions by which three characters?)

Impressions of Winston and Julia

1   What does her arranging of meetings with Winston show of Julia's character?

2   Why is Winston surprised that Julia finds him attractive?

3   Why is Winston pleased when he hears that Julia has had many lovers?

4   Why is the bird's song significant to Winston and Julia?

5   What evidence is there that Goldstein's book is not as important to Julia as it is to Winston?

Whose actions? When?

1   looking at flowers in a disused quarry

2   picking a bunch of bluebells

3   throwing a shoe across a room

4   giving Winston his address

5   bursting through Charrington's window

Text commentary

Part III – Chapters I to VI

Chapter I

> **‟** *He did not know where he was* **”**

Winston is <u>imprisoned</u> in the Ministry of Love, but he does not know how long he has been there or what time of day it is, since there are <u>no windows</u> and the <u>light</u> is on constantly. These factors deliberately confuse and unsettle the inmates. Winston is not referred to directly by name for the first five paragraphs, which adds to the effect of <u>depersonalising</u> the prisoners. He has had nothing to eat since his arrest.

Before being transferred to this cell, Winston was in one containing mainly <u>prole prisoners</u>. He notices the different ways in which the two types are treated and that 'the Party prisoners were always silent and terrified'. One prole woman, 'an enormous wreck of a woman', is also called Smith, and Winston ponders over her suggestion that she might be <u>his mother</u>. Suspense is built when he first hears of <u>Room 101</u>, which gradually becomes more important and mysterious.

> **‟** *He thought oftener of O'Brien, with a flickering of hope* **”**

Winston has plenty of time to think, about food, torture, Julia, O'Brien – even about the chance that a razor blade will be smuggled in to him so that he can commit suicide. He realises that he is now in '<u>the place with no darkness</u>', but the light represents despair rather than hope. The poet <u>Ampleforth</u> and his neighbour <u>Parsons</u> are brought in, even though Parsons was the model citizen.

Winston witnesses <u>extreme</u> <u>brutality</u> from one of the officers towards a prisoner, <u>J Bumstead</u>, who has tried to give a piece of bread to a starving inmate with a 'skull-like' face. When the starving man is collected to go to Room 101, he violently protests, even offering that his whole family be murdered in front of him if he can be spared this fate. This foreshadows Winston's betrayal of Julia when faced with the horrors of Room 101.

<u>O'Brien</u> arrives and Winston presumes that he has been 'got' by the Thought Police. O'Brien's punning reply '<u>They got me long ago</u>' forces him to accept that O'Brien is a key member of the Inner Party and entirely <u>loyal</u> to them. Have we been given any reason to suspect O'Brien? A guard attacks Winston with a truncheon, which removes any shadow of doubt about O'Brien's position of power.

Chapter II

> **66** *Now the turning point has come. I shall save you* **99**

Winston's lengthy <u>brainwashing</u> begins, stage-managed by O'Brien, who is the only one Winston sees, apart from a man in a white coat with a syringe. He has been <u>interrogated</u> and <u>tortured</u> for an unknown period, falling in and out of consciousness, and has had to confess to many crimes. O'Brien is seen paradoxically as his <u>'tormentor', 'inquisitor', 'protector' and 'friend'</u>. This links with Winston's earlier mixed feelings about him, not knowing whether he could trust him or not, but still feeling drawn to him. O'Brien administers 'a wave of pain' from a machine whenever he does not cooperate. He tries to persuade Winston that he is 'mentally deranged', but can be cured by giving up his deluded ideas.

> **66** *Whatever the Party hold to be truth, is truth* **99**

Winston begins to feel defeated by **doublethink**, when O'Brien tries to convince him that the past and memories only exist as dictated by the Party. The only 'truth' is what the Party says has happened and it is up to each individual to control his memory to keep in line with this. Winston must begin by learning to agree that sometimes $2 + 2 = 5$. Although O'Brien inflicts great pain on Winston, he is described in a **fatherly** way: 'the heavy arm round his shoulders' comforts Winston, who sees him as his '**protector**'; he speaks 'gently' to Winston, who 'blubbered' and 'clung to him like a baby'. This is ironic, since bonds between parent and child are discouraged by the Party. O'Brien explains that Winston is not there to be punished, but to be made sane before he is put to death. He uses historical examples to explain to Winston why this procedure is necessary.

Winston is allowed to ask questions, and he learns that Julia has readily betrayed him. He is not told what is in Room 101, because O'Brien says he already knows, building **suspense** in an otherwise static chapter.

Chapter III

> **The rule of the Party is for ever**

This chapter deals with the **second phase** of Winston's re-integration into the Party, that of understanding. He has completed the **learning** stage and has yet to undergo **acceptance**. Time has passed and he is receiving fewer painful shocks from the machine.

Explore

Research Orwell's views on Nazi Germany and Communist Russia.

O'Brien admits that he co-wrote Goldstein's book, and that its suggestion that the proles will overthrow the Party is complete nonsense. Winston is surprised to hear that '**the Party seeks power entirely for its own sake**' and is not interested in any nobler motive. O'Brien is **fanatical** and

<u>persuasive</u>, because he is so <u>confident</u> in his beliefs, but Orwell enables us to keep his arguments in perspective by making him deny scientifically proven facts that a modern reader would know. What <u>rhetorical</u> <u>devices</u> does O'Brien use to make his speech effective?

> **❝***If you want a picture of the future, imagine a boot stamping on a human face – for ever***❞**

Winston argues that this <u>society</u> <u>cannot</u> <u>survive</u> <u>without</u> <u>love</u> because it would have no life force, and that it will be overcome by the spirit of man. He sees himself as <u>morally</u> <u>superior</u> to the Party. In response to this, O'Brien humiliates him by playing the tape in which Winston had promised to do barbaric deeds to support the Brotherhood, and by making him remove his clothes to see what a feeble, skeletal, unattractive specimen he has become – 'a bag of filth', according to O'Brien, who says he only has himself to blame. Winston's <u>loss</u> <u>of</u> <u>pride</u> is not total though, because he has not betrayed Julia, in the sense that he still loves her. O'Brien understands this, which makes Winston feel 'peculiar reverence' for him – a phrase with religious overtones – despite everything that O'Brien believes and has inflicted on him.

O'Brien is frightening and <u>menacing</u> in this chapter, partly because Orwell compares him and Winston to teacher and pupil (and the menace is highlighted as Orwell shows the lunacy of what O'Brien is trying to teach). He has tremendous <u>power</u> and abuses it. His voice, like the guard's truncheon, 'battered' Winston and his words 'crushed him like a bludgeon'. He can read Winston's mind and refers to the '<u>drama</u>' he has played out with Winston over 7 years. Winston is a <u>puppet</u>, who only had the illusion of acting independently. It is as if the strings were pulled in when it suited the Inner Party to arrest him.

Chapter IV

> **❝** *For 7 years the Party had watched him like a beetle under a magnifying glass* **❞**

Considerable <u>time</u> <u>has</u> <u>passed,</u> for Winston is gaining weight and strength and is living in better conditions, but he is still in a prison cell. He is no longer being tortured and has pleasant dreams. He has virtually given in to the Party, realising that resistance is useless. He sets himself challenges to think along Party lines, all the time wondering when he will be shot.

Although his <u>mind</u> is now in tune with the Party, his <u>heart</u> is not, for he still loves Julia. This is shown when he <u>dreams</u> of the Golden Country and cries out her name. He immediately knows that he will be punished and that he must hide his secrets, even from himself; he must 'feel right' and 'dream right'. He uses a simile to describe his hatred as 'a kind of cyst'. This reminds us

of his varicose ulcer, which is an externalised form of his dissatisfaction. He wants to die hating Big Brother, to show he has beaten the Party. Because Winston tells O'Brien that he hates Big Brother, he is sent on 'the last step' of his journey through prison – to <u>Room</u> <u>101</u>.

Chapter V

> **❝** *The thing that is in Room 101 is the worst thing in the world* **❞**

Explore

How does Winston betray his worst fear? What do you think Julia's might be?

Winston is in Room 101, strapped tightly to a chair. O'Brien explains to him that 'the worst thing' differs from person to person, but in Winston's case it is rats. Two <u>rats</u>, in a divided wire cage with a <u>mask</u> attached to it, are on a table and it dawns on him with horror that the mask will be put over his face. <u>Suspense</u> is maintained here, because at first his view of the rats is blocked. He says he will do anything to avoid this 'unendurable' experience, as O'Brien, in his 'schoolmasterish manner', focuses on the carnivorous behaviour of rats. The cage is moved closer to Winston and the rats become more excited, sensing their prey. Suddenly Winston realises that there is only one way to save himself: 'he must interpose another human being ... between himself and the rats'. As the mask is manoeuvred over him and the cage door is drawing ever closer, he **betrays** **Julia** **totally**, and escapes the rats by yelling that her face should be torn off and her body stripped to the bone in place of his.

Chapter VI

"He could never fix his mind on any one subject for more than a few moments at a time"

Explore

What is the significance of the chess Winston now plays in the café?

The scene moves to the **Chestnut** **Tree** **Café**. Orwell repeats sentences from Part I, Chapter VII, including the very specific '**It** **was** **the** **lonely** **hour** **of** **fifteen**' (this was the time of his first meeting with Julia). It is as though he has come **full** **circle** and it cannot be long before he is shot. He is a regular customer at the café. He does a token amount of work, but he is largely able to come and go as he pleases, for he is now no threat to society. **Victory** **Gin**, which he finds increasingly 'horrible', is what keeps him going: 'It was his life, his death and his resurrection.' He is an alcoholic and the name of the gin suggests a cruel joke by the Party – they have certainly beaten Winston.

"Something was killed in your breast: burnt out, cauterised out"

Winston's attitude has completely changed, for he now absorbs news from the **telescreen** about the war with interest and without scepticism. The passage in brackets: '**(Oceania** **was** **at** **war** **with** **Eurasia;** **Oceania** **had** **always** **been** **at** **war**

with <u>Eurasia)'</u> reads like a <u>chant</u> learned parrot-fashion, showing the reader the falseness of Winston's conversion and how he has been <u>brainwashed</u>. Watching the pictures of the Eurasian army, they remind him of insects 'swarming' and 'a column of ants'. This is reminiscent of his description of the proles, the sector of society which might overthrow the Party.

❝ *I betrayed you* ❞

Winston has bumped into Julia in the <u>park</u>, 'on a vile, biting day in March', where they walk through a <u>bleak</u> <u>landscape</u> of 'ragged leafless shrubs'. Her name is not mentioned so she is depersonalised and the setting is in complete contrast to the warm sunshine of the 'Golden Country' where they met in Part II. Here crocuses have been '<u>dismembered</u> <u>by</u> <u>the</u> <u>wind</u>'. The verb suggests that even nature has been ripped apart and dissected. Julia has changed and looks at him with 'contempt and dislike'. They agree that after you have betrayed someone in Room 101 'you don't feel the same towards the other person any longer'.

Winston remembers a happy time with his mother, shortly before she disappeared, but dismisses it as '<u>a</u> <u>false</u> <u>memory</u>'. When the telescreen bulletin announces a tremendous victory in Africa, Winston reacts ecstatically. This marks the moment that the changes wrought on him in the Ministry of Love are complete. In a 'blissful dream' he imagines being shot; gone are his earlier hopes of a final protest. The novel ends, as it began, with a focus on the poster of Big Brother. Winston has found some peace and has conquered his demons; he loves Big Brother, but at what cost?

Appendix – the principles of Newspeak

> **" Newspeak was designed, not to extend but to 'diminish' the range of thought "**

This section expands on the explanation of Newspeak, Oceania's official language, given by Winston's colleague, language expert Syme, in Part I Chapter V. (By Part II Chapter V he has been vaporized, despite being a genuine enthusiast of Newspeak, which perhaps does not give much hope for the survival of the language.) The American Book of the Month Club wanted to publish the novel on condition that Orwell removed both this section and that on Goldstein's book in Part II. Orwell would not hear of this.

Explore

Why do you think Orwell considered this section to be so important? Have you read it?

We learn that in the year 1984 Newspeak was still developing and was not expected to take over fully from Standard English until the mid-twenty-first century. It was devised so that all citizens could express the ideas of Ingsoc (English Socialism) and would not be able to voice any thoughts which ran counter to its beliefs. This aim would be achieved partly by inventing new words, such as '**sexcrime**' (which was used as the title of the Eurythmics' theme song for the 1984 film version of the novel) and '**duckspeak**', but mainly by removing 'undesirable' words from the language. Vocabulary was divided into three classes, A, B and C, according to function, with B being the key group of political and what we would now call 'politically correct' words. Newspeak grammar was very regular, which fits in with the principle of everyone having to do everything along strict guidelines in every aspect of life. Great works of literature – such as those you study for GCSE perhaps – were to be translated into Newspeak and the original versions destroyed. Anything in them which spoke of personal freedom, love and honourable emotions would obviously be removed. (Imagine the effect this would have on plays such as *Romeo and Juliet*.)

It is interesting to consider who is meant to be the author of this section. It may be written as if by Orwell, to further his reader's understanding, or has he assumed the character of a future historian, writing about Newspeak after its collapse? The last suggestion is indicated by the use of past tense: 'The grammar of Newspeak *had* two outstanding peculiarities.' Certainly when we read that 'It was expected that Newspeak *would have* superseded Oldspeak... by about the year 2050', it sounds as if this aim was not achieved. If it had been successful, noone would have been able to write so analytically about Newspeak because the language to accomplish this would have been destroyed. Analytical thinking and writing was not permitted by the Party, as we know from the main body of the novel. We must deduce that the reign of Big Brother ended before 2050. Even though it was too late for Winston to appreciate it there is, after all, a faint glimmer of hope at the end of *Nineteen Eighty-Four*.

Explore

Can you speak Newspeak?

1 What is Minipax?

2 Who are the Thinkpol?

3 What is Standard English for 'uncold'?

4 How do you say 'very good' and 'superlatively good'?

5 Translate the adverb 'speedwise'.

Quick questions

1   Where is Winston being kept prisoner?

2   Why doesn't he know what time of day it is?

3   Which colleagues join him in the cell?

4   What do fellow prisoners seem to fear most?

5   Who interrogates Winston?

6   How many stages of re-integration into the Party are there?

7   What does Winston drink in the café?

8   Who does he love, by the end of the novel?

A process of elimination

1   Parsons is betrayed to the Thought Police by his wife/his son/his daughter.

2   O'Brien is compared to a soldier/a teacher/a politician.

3   Winston meets Julia in the park/the café/Victory Square.

4   In the café Winston plays cards/chess/snakes and ladders.

Complete the quotations

1   'We shall meet in the place where there is no _____.' (O'Brien)

2   'Two and two make _____.' (Party brainwashing)

3   'Freedom is _____.' (Party slogan)

4   'Imagine a _____ stamping on a _____ for ever.' (O'Brien)

5   'Do it to _____!' (Winston)

Impressions of Winston

1   What are the main physical changes in Winston as a result of his torture?

2   Why does he feel such respect for O'Brien?

3   What does Julia now think about him?

4   Why does he betray Julia in Room 101?

5   What is his attitude towards his own death?

Writing essays for exams and coursework

Exams

- To prepare for an exam, you should read the text in full at least twice, preferably three times. You need to know it very well.

- If your text is to be studied for an 'open book' exam, make sure that you take it with you! However, you should not rely too much on the book – you haven't got time. If you are not allowed to take the text with you, you will need to memorise brief quotations.

- You need to decide fairly swiftly about which question to answer. Choose a question which best allows you to demonstrate your understanding and personal ideas.

- Make sure you understand exactly what the question is asking you to do.

- **Plan** your answer (see later section).

- Always have a short introduction, giving an overview of the topic. Refer to your plan as you write to ensure you keep on task. Divide your ideas into paragraphs; without them you may not get above a D. Try to leave time for a brief conclusion.

- Remember: **point–quotation–comment:** Julia is young and healthy [**point**] and reminds Winston of 'community hikes' and 'hockey fields' [**quotation**]. This makes her sound as if she is energetic and supports the Party [**comment**].

- The key word in writing essays in exams is **timing**. You must know how long you have for each question and stick to this.

- Leave yourself a few minutes to check through your work. It does not look impressive if you misspell the names of characters, settings or the author himself.

- Timing is not so crucial for coursework essays, so this is your chance to show what you can really do, without having to write under pressure.

- You can obviously go into far more detail than you are able to in an examination. You should aim for about 1000 words, but your teacher will advise you further.

- If you have a choice of title, make sure you select one that grabs your interest and gives you a lot of opportunity to develop your ideas.

- **Plan** your work (see later section). Make sure that you often refer to the plan and the title as you write, to check that you are not drifting off course.

- Use quotations frequently but carefully and try to introduce them smoothly. It is often effective to quote just one or two words.

- Try to state your own opinion with phrases such as 'This suggests to me…'. You will be credited for your ideas, as long as you explain why you think them.

- Putting the novel in context is very important. Include relevant background detail and explain how the cultural and historical setting affects the writer's choice of language.

- Make sure that you include a short conclusion, summing up your key ideas.

- Don't be tempted to copy large chunks of essays available on the Internet. Your teacher will immediately notice what you have done and will not reward it.

- It is a good idea, if possible, to word process your essay. This will enable you to make changes and improvements to your final draft more easily.

Writing essays

Key quotations

> **Big Brother is watching you**

(Chapter I) Slogan written on posters of Big Brother. Use as evidence of totalitarianism, lack of freedom and omnipotence of the State. (Language features: use of present tense, personal pronoun 'you' and alliteration.)

> **WAR IS PEACE, FREEDOM IS SLAVERY, IGNORANCE IS STRENGTH**

(Chapters I, II and VIII) Slogans of the Party. Use as evidence of totalitarianism, lack of freedom and 'doublethink'. (Language features: always written in capitals, balanced sentences and use of paradox.)

> **Nothing was your own except the few cubic centimetres inside your skull**

(Chapter II) Believed by Winston. Use as evidence of Winston's character, lack of freedom, lack of privacy, totalitarianism. (Language features: use of precise measurement, 'skull' imagery hints at death.)

> **If there is hope it lies in the proles**

(Chapter VII but used throughout Parts I and II) Written initially by Winston in his diary. Use as evidence of totalitarianism, Winston's character, vision of the future, socialism. (Language features: use of present tense, although it later becomes past tense. Also, 'if' suggests only a tentative belief in salvation.)

❝Of all the horrors in the world – a rat!❞

(Part II, Chapter IV) Spoken by Winston in Charrington's room. Use to support essay on horror, violence, nature, dreams, Winston's character. It also links to Room 101. (Language features: use of exclamation mark, hyperbole, key word at the end of the sentence.)

❝If you want a picture of the future, imagine a boot stamping on a human face – forever.❞

(Part III, Chapter III) Spoken by O'Brien to Winston. Use to support essay on totalitarianism, violence, Party control, lack of freedom. (Language features: use of dynamic verb 'stamping', 'forever' suggests lack of hope and eternal Party rule.)

❝The atmosphere of hockey-fields and cold baths and community hikes and general clean-mindedness❞

(Part I, Chapter I) Description of Julia. Use as evidence of Julia's character, Party control. (Language features: listing, interesting adjectives, such as 'cold', 'community' and 'clean', connection with school.)

❝He had the air of a doctor, a teacher, even a priest❞

(Part III, Chapter II) Description of O'Brien. Use to support essay on the character of O'Brien, Party control and indoctrination. The quotation illustrates how Big Brother infiltrates any position of trust and power.

Exam questions

1. *Explore to what extent* Nineteen Eighty-Four *is a warning against totalitarianism.*

2. *In what ways is* Nineteen Eighty-Four *a terrifying vision for the future?*

3. *What is the role played by the proles in* Nineteen Eighty-Four?

4. *Explain how Orwell presents the idea of power in its various forms.*

5. *In what ways is Chapter I an effective opening to the novel?*

6. *Discuss the significance and nature of Winston's dreams. How do these develop our understanding of life under Big Brother?*

7. *Is Winston an heroic figure? What qualities does he possess that could define him as one?*

8. *Julia, a 'rebel from the waist down'. How far do you agree with this statement?*

9. *Discuss the role of relationships and love in* Nineteen Eighty-Four.

10. *Winston argues that the 'spirit of man' can defeat a society such as that created by the Party. How far is this statement justified by the events of the novel?*

11. *Discuss why the past is of such importance to Winston.*

12. *Imagine you are Julia at the end of the novel. Write a letter to Winston, explaining what happened to you in Room 101 and why you can no longer see him.*

13. *'This is among the most terrifying books I have read.' How far do you agree with this comment on the novel?*

14. *You are Parsons – write a letter to your wife from prison telling her how you have been treated and explaining how you feel about your arrest.*

15 *Violence is a theme that runs through the novel. What kinds of violence does Orwell depict and how does he use language to depict it?*

16 *You are O'Brien – write your thoughts after the visit of Winston and Julia to your home. Include:*
   - *what your future plans are regarding Winston*
   - *how well you think your strategy is working*
   - *your thoughts about Julia.*

17 *Orwell uses language to great effect in the novel. Choose two incidents you think are particularly powerful and explain how the language is used to create effect.*

18 *Which character do you find most memorable in the novel? Justify your choice, with close reference to the text.*

19 *Explore how Orwell uses propaganda as a theme in the novel. Why would it be so important in the society of 1984?*

20 *'If there is hope it lies with the proles.' Do you feel any glimmer of hope at the end of the novel?*

21 *How are women presented by Orwell in* Nineteen Eighty-Four?

22 *Orwell uses setting to good effect in* Nineteen Eighty-Four. *Compare the 'Golden Country' with the real-life setting of London.*

Passage-based questions

If you are required to answer a question based on an extract from the novel in the exam, make sure you focus on the language used, and also refer to other examples from the rest of the novel. After reading the extract, highlight key phrases to help you write your response.

Planning an essay

It is very important to be organised in your approach. Time spent in planning your response will be reflected in the grade you receive.

- The first thing to do is to read the question very carefully to make sure you fully understand it and then highlight key words.

- You will need to make some notes on the topic to help you. This can be done in various ways: a list; subheadings; spidergram; or a mind map.

- The advantage of using a spidergram is that it lets you expand your ideas in a clearly linked, visual way. Put the essay title in the centre of the page. From this a number of key ideas will come out in the form of branches.

- By focusing on each key idea in turn, you will be able to branch out further, as your brain makes connections between the ideas.

- Since mind maps and spidergrams are ways of charting your knowledge, they are also excellent revision aids. You could work through a number of essay titles in this way.

- Some people prefer to make a mind map even more visual, by colour coding ideas and even adding pictures or symbols.

- In the planning stage of an essay it is also a good idea to jot down some useful quotations. These need not be lengthy and can be added to your mind map.

- Each branch of a mind map might form a separate paragraph in your essay. You can number the branches, so that you are clear about the order of your points. Deal with the main points first.

- Some pupils say that they do not like planning and that they never do so, but the majority of candidates do significantly better when they plan their answers.

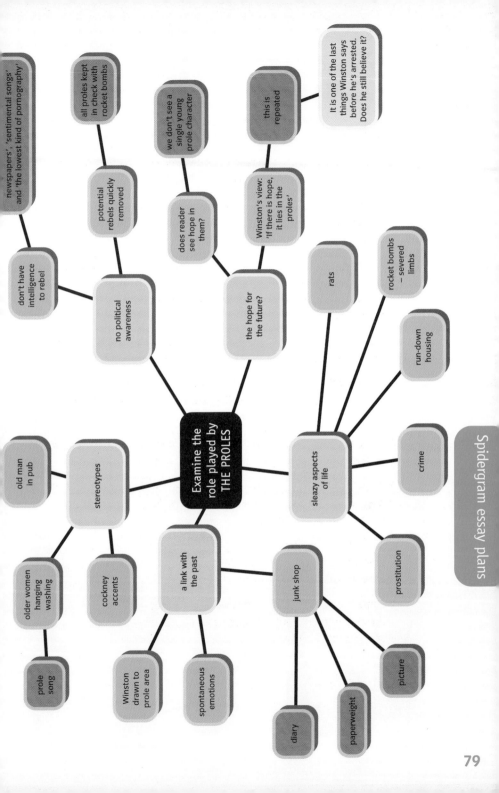

Examine the role played by THE PROLES

no political awareness
- don't have intelligence to rebel
- potential rebels quickly removed
  - all proles kept in check with rocket bombs
  - newspapers', 'sentimental songs' and 'the lowest kind of pornography'

the hope for the future?
- does reader see hope in them?
- we don't see a single young prole character
- Winston's view: 'If there is hope, it lies in the proles'
  - this is repeated
    - It is one of the last things Winston says before he's arrested. Does he still believe it?

stereotypes
- old man in pub
- cockney accents
- older women hanging washing
  - prole song

a link with the past
- Winston drawn to prole area
- spontaneous emotions
- junk shop
  - diary
  - paperweight
  - picture

sleazy aspects of life
- rats
- rocket bombs – severed limbs
- run-down housing
- crime
- prostitution

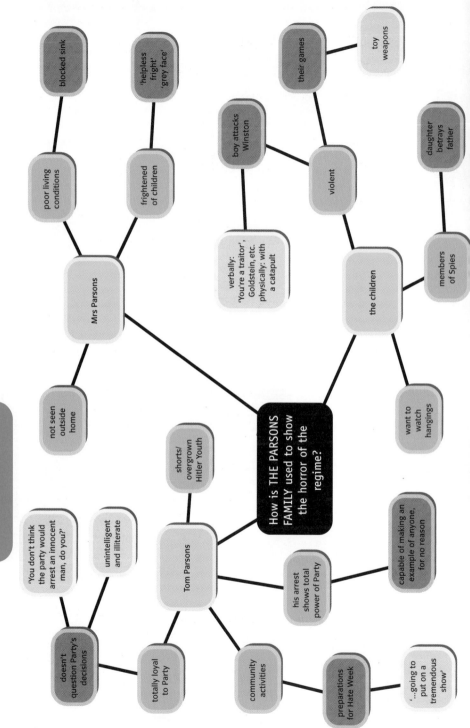

How is THE PARSONS FAMILY used to show the horror of the regime?

Mrs Parsons
- poor living conditions
  - blocked sink
- frightened of children
  - 'helpless fright' 'grey face'
- not seen outside home

the children
- their games
  - toy weapons
- violent
  - boy attacks Winston
    - verbally: 'You're a traitor', Goldstein, etc. physically: with a catapult
- members of Spies
  - daughter betrays father
- want to watch hangings

Tom Parsons
- shorts/ overgrown Hitler Youth
- his arrest shows total power of Party
  - capable of making an example of anyone, for no reason
- community activities
  - preparations for Hate Week
    - '...going to put on a tremendous show'
- totally loyal to Party
- doesn't question Party's decisions
  - 'You don't think the party would arrest an innocent man, do you?'
  - unintelligent and illiterate

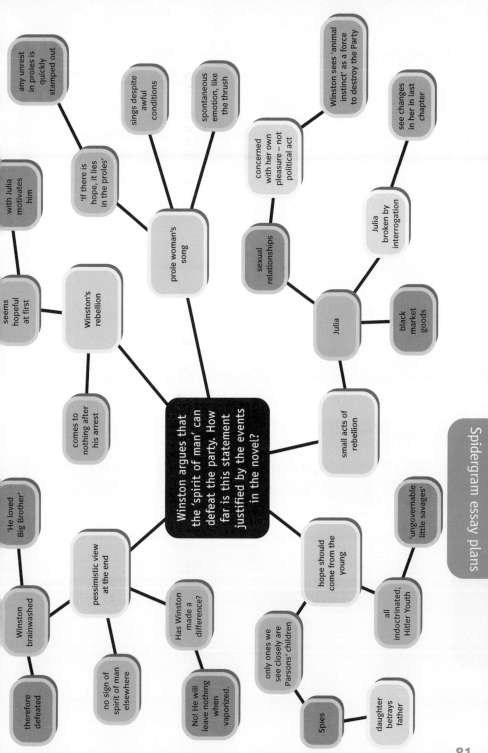

Winston argues that the 'spirit of man' can defeat the party. How far is this statement justified by the events in the novel?

Winston's rebellion
- any unrest in proles is quickly stamped out
- 'If there is hope, it lies in the proles'
- with Julia motivates him
- seems hopeful at first
- comes to nothing after his arrest

prole woman's song
- sings despite awful conditions
- spontaneous emotion, like the thrush

sexual relationships
- concerned with her own pleasure – not political act
- Winston sees 'animal instinct' as a force to destroy the Party

Julia
- see changes in her in last chapter
- Julia broken by interrogation
- black market goods

small acts of rebellion

pessimistic view at the end
- 'He loved Big Brother'
- Winston brainwashed
- therefore defeated
- no sign of spirit of man elsewhere
- Has Winston made a difference?
- No! He will leave nothing when vaporized.

hope should come from the young
- 'ungovernable little savages'
- all indoctrinated; Hitler Youth
- only ones we see closely are Parsons' children
- Spies
- daughter betrays father

Sample response

How does Orwell present a depressing picture of the world in which Winston is living in the opening of *Nineteen Eighty-Four*?

The start of the book is very depressing because the weather is cold and because Winston seems very miserable. It also says 'the clocks were striking thirteen', which is unusual. It feels like everything is grey and dirty. ✔ The setting is also depressing because everything is broken or destroyed, maybe because of age or a war: '...these vistas of rotting nineteenth-century houses, their sides shored up with baulks of timber, their windows patched with cardboard and their roofs with corrugated iron, their crazy garden walls sagging in all directions.' ✔

Winston does not seem very happy with his life because he is getting older and he has an ulcer on his right ankle, 'a varicose ulcer above his right ankle'. ✔ In the building where he lives nothing works properly, like the lift and even the electricity is cut off during the day, which means that it is harder getting up stairs.

In 1984 there is no freedom. Orwell wrote 'Nineteen Eighty-Four' as a warning and he wanted people to realise what life would be like if there was no democracy or freedom. ✔ There are posters everywhere of Big Brother and these posters tell you 'Big Brother is Watching You'. This shows that there is no privacy because there is always someone watching your every movement, and you can't get away with anything. ✔

Winston's room has a telescreen in it which means that he is never alone and always watched by the 'Thought Police'. These are a brutal army-like squad of policemen who make sure that the population behaves properly and does not do anything that would go against Big Brother. ✓ Everyone has a telescreen in their home and there are hundreds all over the place, which remind me of eyes, trained to spot when people are doing something wrong. This is another example of why life is so depressing. ✓

The people of Oceania are not even allowed to watch what they want because they have to listen to details about how much 'pig-iron' has been produced. This shows how little freedom the people have and how the government makes sure they are doing the right things. ✓

Overall life is very depressing because nothing works properly, the weather is not very cheerful, Winston is quite ill and Big Brother has total control over the population so you would not be able to breathe without someone watching your every move. ✓

Examiner's comments

This is a solid response which shows good understanding of the novel and cultural context. The candidate demonstrates insight into how meaning and ideas are conveyed through language, and refers to textual evidence to support views. Quotations are not always developed and the response could be more exploratory in places. It is rather simplistic. The essay has a good, clear structure and the candidate attempts to remain focused on the title. There is a neat conclusion. Overall, this is an accurate, pleasing, if slightly under-developed, response to the question.

Sample response

How does Orwell present a depressing picture of the world in which Winston is living in the opening of _Nineteen Eighty-Four_?

At once, when reading the very start of the novel, the reader is confronted by a typical, almost clichéd depressing image. The clocks are 'striking thirteen' in the very first sentence. ✔ The number thirteen is shrouded in a myth of horror and bad luck, derived from the Last Supper in the Bible. This depressing start is emphasised more by the pathetic fallacy of 'bright cold day.' ✔ There are other examples of description creating a depressing atmosphere, such as 'gritty dust', 'grimy landscape' and 'there seemed to be no colour in anything'. These images increase and emphasise the scene's desolation and bleakness. ✔

Another way in which Orwell creates a depressing scene is the constant references to destruction and decay: '...these vistas of rotting nineteenth-century houses, their sides shored up with baulks of timber, their windows patched with cardboard and their roofs with corrugated iron, their crazy garden walls sagging in all directions'. These suggest that the world has become ravaged and ruined by war and is on the point of collapse. ✔ The scene is described brilliantly by Orwell, creating images of slums or the remains of London, after the Second World War, something Orwell would have seen for himself. It is not only the setting that is decaying, of course. Even Winston himself suffers from a perpetual sore on his leg, a 'varicose ulcer'. ✔✔

Perhaps, though, what is most depressing in the extract, indeed throughout the entire novel, is the distinct lack of individual rights, freedom and liberty. Orwell wrote 'Nineteen Eighty-Four' as a warning to mankind at the time of his writing it, trying to explain that democracy and freedom could easily be destroyed if dictators were allowed to take control. ✔

Orwell shows his readers this vision by including many examples of dictatorship, slavery and oppression, even in the opening chapter. He writes,

'The police patrol snooping into people's windows.' Obviously Winston's world is one with very little privacy. The repetition of 'BIG BROTHER IS WATCHING YOU', with its use of present tense suggesting that there is no escape and the ever-apparent posters create an uncomfortable sense of paranoia on the part of Winston and the reader. ✔ The passage ends: 'every sound you made was overheard ... every movement scrutinised.' The use of the word 'scrutinised' is important, because this is more than just being watched. It means you are being examined thoroughly, in the way that evidence after a crime would be minutely scrutinised. ✔✔ In 'Nineteen Eighty-Four' the Party is waiting for you to commit a crime.

The worst form of oppression voiced in this passage, though, is the small term 'Thought Police'. ✔ Winston is living in a world where even people's thoughts are controlled and freedom of thought is the most basic human right. Total lack of control is depressing beyond belief and that, combined with the colourless, desolate and derelict world Winston lives in, creates the emotions of pure desperation and depression. ✔

Examiner's comments

This is a thoughtful and sophisticated response, which demonstrates an excellent understanding of the novel's social and historical context. The candidate consistently reveals insight into how meaning and ideas are conveyed through language, and refers to textual evidence to support views. Comments are often original and connections between ideas are made. Quotations are always accompanied by further comment and high-level language terminology is used throughout. The essay is well structured and there is a conclusion, although time constraints have meant that this is a little abrupt. Overall, this is very accurate, and suggests a candidate who has engaged well with the text and thoroughly understands the way a writer uses language and form to create desired effects.

Quick quiz answers

Quiz 1

Quick questions
1. April
2. Big Brother
3. a diary
4. to unblock the sink
5. the Parsons boy
6. Syme
7. Julia
8. Winston's wife (they are separated)
9. rocket bombs
10. a glass paperweight

A process of elimination
1. Airstrip One
2. The Ministry of Truth
3. O'Brien's
4. Mrs Parsons
5. Charrington

Complete the quotations
1. thirteen
2. proles (Winston says this)
3. peace
4. four
5. chop off your head

Impressions of Winston
1. He dislikes almost all women, especially young ones.
2. It is his greatest pleasure in life.
3. He dreams about it.
4. He thinks O'Brien is someone he could talk to who may share similar views.
5. It makes him feel nostalgic and secure.

Who is this?
1. Winston
2. O'Brien
3. Big Brother
4. Goldstein
5. Parsons
6. Julia
7. Mrs Parsons
8. Katharine
9. Charrington
10. Parsons boy

Quiz 2

Quick questions
1. The Thought Police
2. The Fiction Department in the Ministry of Truth
3. chocolate
4. scarlet
5. the prole woman who hangs out washing
6. Parsons
7. a dictionary (later he lends him Goldstein's book)
8. O'Brien's servant
9. The Brotherhood
10. black

A process of elimination
1. a corridor
2. thrush
3. Syme
4. the past
5. in Charrington's room

Complete the quotations
1. love
2. rat (Winston says this)
3. strength
4. Country
5. dead (Winston, O'Brien and Julia all say this)

Impressions of Winston and Julia
1 her organisation ('military precision'), initiative, fearlessness, rebelliousness
2 He is bit of a physical wreck, has a wife, and is much older than Julia.
3 He thinks it might indicate that the Party is rotten under the surface. ('Anything that hinted at corruption always filled him with a wild hope.')
4 The bird sings spontaneously, without an apparent reason, just for itself. It doesn't follow rules. It fascinates them and relaxes Winston ('He stopped thinking and merely felt).
5 Julia falls asleep when Winston reads from it! Her rebellion is one of the senses rather than the intellect.

Whose actions? When?
1 Winston and Katharine, when they got lost while on a community hike.
2 Winston, for Julia, before meeting her in the wood.
3 Julia, when she sees a rat in Charrington's room.
4 O'Brien, when he meets Winston in the corridor, by a telescreen.
5 The Thought Police, when they come to arrest Winston and Julia.

Quiz 3
Quick questions
1 in the Ministry of Love
2 there are no windows or clocks; the lights are on all the time

3 Ampleforth and Parsons
4 Room 101
5 O'Brien
6 three (learning; understanding; acceptance)
7 gin
8 Big Brother

A process of elimination
1 his daughter
2 a teacher
3 the park
4 chess

Complete the quotations
1 darkness
2 five
3 slavery
4 a) boot b) human face
5 Julia

Impressions of Winston
1 Winston is thinner, is partly bald and has lost some teeth.
2 He feels that O'Brien understands him.
3 Julia no longer loves him; she feels contempt and dislike for him.
4 When faced with the rats, his worst fear, he has no option.
5 He is looking forward to it; he entirely accepts it.

Can you speak Newspeak?
1 The Ministry of Peace
2 Thought Police
3 warm
4 plusgood; doubleplusgood
5 quickly

Page 18, George Orwell, ©Corbis Sygma
Page 21 scene, ©E.O. Hoppé/Corbis

First published 2004

Letts Educational
Chiswick Centre
414 Chiswick High Road
London W4 5TF
Tel: 020 8996 3333

Text © Clare Crane and Juliet Walker 2004

Cover and text design by Hardlines Ltd., Charlbury, Oxfordshire.

Typeset by Letterpart Ltd., Reigate, Surrey.

Graphic illustration by Beehive Illustration, Cirencester, Gloucestershire.

Commissioned by Cassandra Birmingham

Editorial project management by Vicky Butt

Printed in Italy.

Design and illustration © Letts Educational Ltd

British Library Cataloguing in Publication Data. A CIP record of this book is available from the British Library.

ISBN 1 84315 325 4

Letts Educational is a division of Granada Learning, part of Granada plc.